STRETCH

Reaching Beyond the Noise

STRETCH

Reaching Beyond the Noise

Judith Greiner Duncan, PhD

XULON PRESS

Xulon Press
2301 Lucien Way #415
Maitland, FL 32751
407.339.4217
www.xulonpress.com

Printed in the United States of America.
ISBN-13: 978-1-54565-499-6

DEDICATION

To my heavenly Father who has generously supplied everything I need and so many of my desires.

To my husband, James, a faithful child of God, an awesome husband and father and a gifted encourager. You have worked quietly in the background to support my quest for knowledge and my desire to make disciples as we minister God's Word together.

To my mother, Helen Spencer Greiner. Mom, you have always put God first and your family a close second; you have nurtured and encouraged my intellectual growth as well as my spiritual pursuits. Thank you for your example of steadfast courage in the face of adversity.

To my son, Larry, who loves God and walks out his faith as he shares his time and resources with many who just need a boost up in their lives. Son, you inspire me and others; may your ministry continue to grow.

To my sisters: Redith, Carol, Linda, and Kathy. Your unswerving love for God and His people inspires others to be all they can be and to attain all God wants them to be.

To the rest of my family: Wilson, Bailey, McKenzie, Cameron, Tracy, Ryan, Tori, Reagan, Emma, Kyleigh and Ellie. You light up my life and enrich me more than you'll ever know.

In memory of Zachary Lynn Duncan
1968–2007

CONTENTS

———◆———

Chapter 1

BEFORE THE BEGINNING

We cannot become what we want to be
by remaining what we are.
–Max DePree

———◆———

S tretch pants.
Stretch marks.
Home stretch.
Stretch for strength and flexibility.

Stretching suggests many different pictures. The beautiful minutes-old baby throwing off the confines of the nine-month home his mother provided. That furry family pet that drags herself out of a nap. The seventh inning stretch in baseball.

While the idea of the stretch carries with it a plethora of images, most of them pleasant, one of the first to capture my mind is women in stretch pants, maybe because I've seen so many of these on the fashion scene during the last few years. Little wonder they're so popular. For the most part, they become wider and expand on bodies that we physically force into them. You see them everywhere. On long and lean bodies, on short and squat bodies, on men and on women. On children. On many physiques that might look better in something else. (Don't people look in full-length mirrors after getting dressed these days?) I can understand why people choose to wear them. They're unbelievably comfortable, almost like a second skin, and warm in the cooler months of the year. Like many others, I suppose, I sacrifice beauty and decorum for comfort and wear them anyway.

To move away from my personal bias quickly, let's look at a different stretch. Trained physicians and physiologists propose that

1

stretching the body has a number of benefits. Done properly and under the correct conditions, stretching can increase flexibility and range of motion; it may prevent or decrease joint pain; it could improve balance. But those same physicians and physiologists say inappropriate physical stretching poses possible dangers: it can increase weakness and instability or even aggravate the underlying conditions that the one who stretches hopes to alleviate. The importance of knowing how to stretch cannot be underestimated. That's true in the spiritual as well as the physical realm.

Artists may think of pulling a canvas taut over a wooden frame as they mentally plan how the finished product might look. Mothers-to-be may look at their growing bellies and pray that the skin there will not be permanently stretched. Professional truck drivers may think of their long journey as a stretch. For financially challenged people, the desire to own their own home seems a stretch. For people who are willing to stretch spiritually, the prospects are monumental. Almost always we have to stretch to deal with circumstances that life hands us and to reach our goals.

All of those stretches are important to someone at one time or another, but I'd like to focus for now on a spiritual possibility. That direction starts with a look at Bible passage that records a very short prayer illustrating one man's desire to be stretched:

> And Jabez was more honourable than his brethren: and his mother called his name Jabez, saying, Because I bare him with sorrow. And Jabez called on the God of Israel, saying, Oh that thou wouldest bless me indeed, and enlarge my coast, and that thine hand might be with me, and that thou wouldest keep me from evil, that it may not grieve me! And God granted him that which he requested (1 Chronicles 4:9–10).

These verses are the only ones in the Bible referring to the man known as Jabez, the man whose name means "sorrow" or "trouble" because his mother experienced pain during his birth. His name gives rise to many questions. Didn't his mother experience pain while giving birth to her other children? Did the pain in the birth of Jabez far outweigh her joy in the new baby boy? Had she just had an argument with her husband before taking the child to the circumcision? How did he feel as he heard his mother calling his name many times a day and knowing that it means "sorrow" or "trouble"?

"Don't cry, Sorrow. Mummy loves you."

"Come and eat, Sorrow."

"Good morning, Trouble. It's time to get up and get ready for school."

"No, Sorrow, you may not hang out with your friends tonight."

How does a child overcome such a handicap? This story doesn't provide a clue. It reveals nothing much about Jabez. Based on the number of words devoted to his example, the man seems somewhat like a baseball player on a sandlot or a farm team. He doesn't get much press. He's not featured in the evening news. He's not pictured on the front cover of a popular magazine. To put him back in context, there's not even a Bible book named for him. His words must be important though. They've been incorporated into the Word of God. This verse says that there's something to be learned from Jabez and his story. Described as "more honorable than his brothers," Jabez prayed to the God of Abraham, Isaac, and Jacob. He prayed a specific prayer that resonates with me and other believers.

"Bless me, enlarge my coast, keep me from evil." These words of Jabez have appealed to Bible readers across the years and especially since Dr. Bruce Wilkinson's book *The Prayer of Jabez: Breaking Through to the Blessed Life* (Multnomah Publishers, 2000) appeared and made the New York Times Bestseller List. Although Dr. Wilkinson's book has inspired mixed reactions, it has encouraged many thousands of people to pray similar prayers. Those reading his prayer will see a man who, many centuries ago, prayed for God to stretch him, to extend his sphere of influence. He just used different terminology as he asked that God bless him, guide him, increase his opportunities for ministry, and keep him from evil that would cause pain.

It is probably safe to say that every true follower of Christ wants God's blessing. The idea of blessing carries with it the act of making holy and fit for use in the kingdom of God as well as making anointing and power for service available. It also speaks to provision for benefits in life: health, financial needs, mental peace, spiritual needs, physical needs and the like—present and future. Through Christ, God has provided all that believers need. They simply receive by faith. The New Testament, the last will and testament of the Lord Jesus, records His promises and provisions. Those provisions are secured by faith in His Word. Jesus said to His disciples, "'What things soever ye desire, when ye pray, believe that ye receive them, and ye shall have them'" (Mark 11:24).

Of course, Jesus attached qualifications to that promise: first, *ask* (pray), then *believe* and, finally, *forgive* anyone that you're holding something against so that your heavenly Father can forgive you (Mark 11:24-25). The Bible also promises through Paul that "God *shall* supply *all* your *need* according to his riches in glory by Christ Jesus." (Philippians 4:19, emphasis added).

You'll get what you ask for if you "really believe it will happen and have no doubt in your heart" (Mark 11:23 NLT) and if you don't have the wrong motives: "Ye ask, and receive not, because ye ask amiss, that ye may consume it upon your lusts" (James 4:3). God has promised, and He will supply every need. If there's any truth to the Bible (and I'm convinced that it's the holy Word of a living God transmitted to us through inspired men of God), you can depend on this promise.

Assured that "the steps of a good man are ordered by the Lord" (Psalm 37:23), we can safely depend on Him to guide our lives. That guidance, more often than not, takes us into new and different realms with which we are not comfortable; it opens up opportunities for life and influence that are large enough to lead us to failure. In every phase of life itself, not just in relationships and careers, we have greater success when we learn to trust God because we recognize His strength and wisdom are far superior to our own. Finally, each one of us who names the name of Christ will want, like Jabez and the naturopathic doctor, to "first do no harm" and "cause no pain."

These are general ideas suggested by the title of this book. As you read, I ask you to keep in mind the notion of growing or being expanded or spread beyond what you might have expected or thought of as normal or usual. That extension, that stretch, can begin at birth and carry through all the years of your life if you submit early in life to the will of God. It can happen for you if you have spent most of your life running from God and pursuing your own plans and dreams. It can begin where you are — even if you're in your golden years — and make a difference in your here and now as well as in your eternity. If you trust God and move as He directs, the stretch will never cause you to be "maxed out" or "burned out." On the contrary, each new challenge creates an opportunity for growth, and the One who promised to direct your steps will give you the energy, the direction, and the authority to complete the growth.

My stretch began many years ago in a very small town in West Virginia. It continues to this day. Sometimes it has been a gentle stretch that kept me from stagnating. Sometimes it has been a challenging pull into spheres where my efforts would absolutely have failed unless and until the God of all creation stepped in and empowered and directed that movement.

Do you dare accept a challenge to revive your long-buried dreams and pursue them? You will be able to move forward if you put your trust in the strength Christ gives you, but you'll have to move out of your comfort zone. You may have to find a new set of friends whose beliefs and passions more closely match your own new ones. You may have to leave behind long-held beliefs and attitudes. You may have to be willing to leave the familiar far behind and sometimes undertake a journey while you don't really know where you're going. This kind of extending and journeying are part of a life that discovers God's purpose and pursues it, a life that is willing to be molded into the image and likeness of Jesus Christ.

Some people in this world choose to go the distance in life without a relationship with Jesus and appear to be very successful. They have money, an abundance of stuff, fine houses with enviable furnishings, prestige, prominence, power—and empty souls. Like the rich young ruler who came to Christ asking what he could do to inherit eternal life, they turn away unfulfilled when they learn that Christ wants those who seek eternal life to *be willing to forsake* everything and follow Him (Matthew 19:16–22). Many are unwilling to take themselves off the throne and give first place to God; they are afraid to put their trust in someone besides themselves. Maybe they are unwilling to recognize that it is God's goodness and mercy that have given them life, physical and mental strength, and the personality traits to become successful in this life. They cheat themselves out of the opportunity to test the Lord and allow Him to use what they have to honor Him and fulfill their God-given destiny on this earth.

The prophet Jeremiah, in the midst of calamity and destruction in Jerusalem, declared, "Great is thy faithfulness" (Lamentations 3:22–24). The keys to knowing God's faithfulness for yourself are (1) to live a God-first life, (2) to trust God in the bad times and the good, (3) to walk with Him and let Him guide you through the challenges of life and (4) to hold on to His promises with a bulldog tenacity.

5

Like many others, I have taken a lifetime to learn that God not only plans our lives but He also equips us for the journey that He sets before us. He sometimes changes our direction in midstream, but we can be assured of His presence and His guidance as we travel. He promised never to leave or forsake His people: "For I the Lord thy God will hold thy right hand, saying unto thee, Fear not; I will help thee . . . I the God of Israel will not forsake them" (Isaiah 41:13, 17).

Just as he was unwilling to forsake His chosen people then, even in the midst of their unfaithfulness and disobedience, He is faithful to His followers today. Believers may come to the point where they are persecuted or otherwise challenged, but Paul assures that they are never forsaken (2 Corinthians 4:9 ESV).

In my life journey, I have learned many things about how God-given desires and challenges of life stretch us and enlarge our borders. I invite you to continue with me as I retrace parts of my journey. I give you fair warning: my story does not lead in a straight path; sometimes it will meander, and sometimes it will flash back to an earlier time. Sometimes it becomes so personal and transparent that I feel like cringing. However, I believe many of the things I've learned can apply to all people and will bless them whether they are young or old, male or female, completely yielded to Christ, on the fence, or somewhere close to the fence.

Chapter 2

THE WHY

In all thy ways acknowledge him,
And he shall direct thy paths.
–Proverbs 3:6

⸺◆⸺

W hy on earth would anyone with a sound mind want to lead a nation? Every leader in the free world, it seems, is a target for hate speech, push back, and opposition of every kind. Their families are fair game for photographers and reporters, and their private lives all the way back into their childhood are splashed across magazines and newspapers and television screens. Many private citizens would simply never consider exposing themselves and their families to such scrutiny and outright harassment. And yet, in 2016, more than 1,700 people filed to run for president in the United States. By May of 2017, just a little more than a year into President Donald Trump's tenure, 129 people had filed to run in the next election to be held in 2020.

Could it be that all aspiring presidents or prime ministers or other national leaders have a huge ego? Could it be that they believe that they, one single person on a mission, can effect change in this country or another one? Do they believe that they have the personal charisma, the ability to negotiate, the ability to keep interests of the country at the forefront of their agenda, the integrity and strength of character to stand for the truth as they see it? Are they guided by behind-the-scenes persons with agendas of their own, be they lobbyists, congressional members fighting to please their constituents and keep their position as national lawmakers and policy makers, or powerful entities who desire to destroy the fabric and function of their nation?

Early in life, I realized that an aspiring president or prime minister or dictator embraces a specific political philosophy and ideology. Sometimes the would-be leaders have an axe to grind (old hillbilly colloquialism). Their public lives quickly give away the nature of their beliefs and their principles of conduct. Could their motivation rest on a huge ego or a sinister plan or neither? Is it possible that they simply have confidence in their abilities because of their successes in other areas of life and the strengths they have been able to develop? I could also ask the same kinds of questions about writers. What makes them tick?

Is it possible that those who aspire to write can be described in the same way? Does our desire to write reveal a huge ego? Do we have something to sell? Do we have an axe to grind or a bone to pick? A quick, somewhat thoughtless answer might be, "Yes, of course." A bit of thought suggests other responses.

Some of us write or aspire to write to share important evidence from careful research; some of us, to entertain; some, to provoke thought; some, to share important life lessons we've learned. In the large scheme of things, a few write to stir others to support specific actions. And then, some writers share my motivation. I am moved, not by a sense of my own importance or by a desire to add to a knowledge base in my area of expertise. Not this time, anyway. I write because the Spirit of God has nudged me again and again. Even though I have resisted for a long time, I now strongly believe God wants me to use all the talents and gifts He gave me, such as they are, to bring Him honor. I recognize that He has brought me to the place where I am today. God has brought me from darkness to light, from sin to right living, from death to life. It is to Him I owe all gratitude because He has loved me and forgiven me in spite of all my spiritual indifferences and failures. To Him belongs whatever honor that my life might bring Him. So I choose to write the story of my life and God's blessings while praying that He will be honored and glorified.

When I first started in earnest to write this book, I had a strong "inner feeling" that the Spirit of God was urging me to write. With that urge, I also had what might have been a selfish desire birthing inside me. I wanted then—and still want, when I breathe my last breath—to leave not only a God-first life but also a written record of my journey from insecurity and dogma to grace and joy as a legacy to my children and grandchildren—those in my biological family as well as those in what I have learned to call my family of choice (spiritual and secular). I also want to encourage those with a dream to pursue it with God's help.

I decided to share some of my life for three reasons: first of all, I want to obey the Lord. Second, and most obviously, I know the subject very well. Finally, I have experienced many calls to stretch outside my comfort zone: some of them by life's circumstances, some by my own aspirations, many of them by God's direct intervention. My experiences may encourage someone else. My story reveals more intimate aspects of my life and those of my family than I ever thought I could possibly share. And yet I will pull back the curtain on a life that has experienced joy, sorrow, realization of dreams, death to dreams, and a journey that has brought me to an understanding of grace and truth. I share with you a life that has caused me to leave my comfort zone many times, one that has disturbed my complacency, one that continues to offer new challenges.

Now, bear with me please. As a child of God who gave her life to the Lord at an early age and has been reading and teaching the Bible for many years, I am confident it is God who has always had a plan for my life. I also know that I've not asked His will to be done or paid attention to His will before moving ahead at times. Instead, I've often made plans and then asked Him to bless what I decided to do. Many of us do the same thing over and over and then have to deal with the consequences of not being in the perfect will of God.

I've learned that He has always had thoughts to give you and me a future and a hope (Jeremiah 29:11). So when life's challenges have tried my faith, I've also discovered that those challenges are common to humankind and that God gives grace to deal with and overcome the challenges. He walks with us through the trials and hardships. He gives the strength to complete the stretch from one victory to another. He never leaves us without the resources to overcome our obstacles and live lives of victory in Christ.

Another desire has also claimed my attention and fueled my momentum. It is my desire to set my Bible teaching record straight and to reach Christian people for whom a religion of Dos and Don'ts is still keeping them from experiencing the freedom and joy of walking in God's grace. As one of them for many years, I hope that my enlightenment will help those who follow my journey and learn about the treasure I continue to unearth as I leave "religion" behind and come to know the truth and understand God's grace better. I want you to understand that you, too, can and should abandon your checklist, that you can learn how to free yourself from religion and enter into a relationship. Through a relationship with the Savior of the world, you can free yourself from a life of doubt, a life of self-reliance, a life of dread, a life of unhealthy fear. You can come to know and love the God who made such freedom possible.

> He's a *God of love,* the God who "so loved the world that He gave His only begotten son that whosoever believeth on him would not perish but have everlasting life" (John 3:16).

> He's a *God of grace,* the same God by whose undeserved and unearned favor we are saved by faith and not our good works: "For by grace are ye saved through faith; and that not of yourselves: it is the gift of God: Not of works, lest any man should boast" (Ephesians 2:8).

> He's a *God who desires relationship* so much that He came to this earth, lived as a man, and gave His life to pay the sin debt for all who will receive by faith His gift of life eternal: "In the beginning was the Word, and the Word was with God, and the Word was God . . . And the word was made flesh, and dwelt among us" (John 1:1, 14).

Months of mental sorting and dealing with a dread of the long road and hard work I knew were ahead passed. After quite a bit of dawdling and organizing my thoughts—what I called preplanning—I began. I dreamed of a published book ready to give as Christmas gifts a couple of years ago. Little did I know that the gestation period for the birth of *Stretch* would be even longer than that of an elephant. Like any mother into her fortieth week (or in the case of elephant mothers, ninety-eighth week) of pregnancy, I am more than ready for this baby to be birthed.

A little more than two years from the thought and inspiration, I continue to write and rewrite. When I remember that others have churned out best sellers in a few weeks, I first want to rake myself over the coals. Then, I remember that God has His own timetable. It does not always match ours. In fact, it rarely does. I have been experiencing a journey into truth. Just when I thought I had reached the truth and started to share it, something happened to derail my progress. Part of that something, I'm now convinced, was divine intervention. God has been helping me to avoid making the same kinds of mistakes that I've made in the past. Those mistakes, in part, evolved from my upbringing and early religious training.

Set apart by God at an early age for teaching the Bible, I was thrust into the position and the experiences with only a minimum of training. I learned to teach using lessons prepared by someone our church fathers believed to be thoroughly trained in Scripture, someone who always agreed with the established doctrines of the church I was part of. Children's lessons first. Then adult materials published in Sunday school quarterlies. Materials that adults in the class, frequently even the teachers, didn't see the need to study before coming to class so the teacher read aloud and asked members of the class to read aloud parts of the lesson material during the class period. Very little sharing of ideas or questions accompanied the reading. How were people to discuss or question ideas they had not yet seen or considered?

So, I followed the example of those older than I in the Lord. With zeal and passion, I taught what others had prepared. I thought because it had been approved by a "committee" of those under whose authority I worked that it must be gospel. While I read the accompanying Bible verses for each lesson, I did not know to ask God to give me interpretation or the insights I needed as a teacher; I simply plunged into a reading and discussion of the lesson as written, believing that the insights shared in the printed lesson must be from God. By the time I had started to teach adult Bible classes in our small home church sanctuary, I had learned some teaching techniques from my university training and experiences in public school classrooms. I tried to inspire study of the lesson during the week and discussions of the material on Sunday mornings. Getting people in the classes, some of them preachers, to stretch with me was often like pulling teeth. A few class members came along more easily than others. Some needed professional (call it divine) intervention. The result of my experiences? I taught only what I learned from others for the next several decades. Without thinking, I perpetuated the religion of my forefathers.

It was not until the mid-1980s that I had my first unsettling enlightenment. A friend and colleague of my husband loaned us sets of cassette tapes recorded by ministers who were not in our denomination but were also Spirit-filled. Listening faithfully to the tapes daily and following up by searching the Scriptures to check what they were preaching, I began to feel born again—for the second time. As I searched the Word of God to make sure they were not leading me astray, I began to understand that every born again believer, even I, could read the Bible and receive from God divine understanding and inspiration along with His anointing to deliver His Word to others as the opportunity presented.

Suddenly, I knew that we do not have to and should not depend solely on mere mortals to receive our only understanding of the Word and pass it on to us. Along the way and as a result of tragedy in my life, I encountered grace, a concept that one or two dear pastors had introduced, a concept that had continually escaped my understanding for too many years. Along with many other Christians, even those who were Bible teachers and preachers, I have struggled to a comprehension of biblical grace. This journey to understanding has taken me more than thirty years, and I'm still learning.

Like a dog with a new bone, I grabbed the message of God's undeserved and unearned favor and determined to share it with my world. That's when the Holy Spirit brought my new project to a screeching halt. After long periods of wondering why I could not move forward and finish this book, He showed me that my understanding of grace was incomplete and unbalanced, possibly even misleading to persons who may have been persuaded to adopt my understanding. Had I gone overboard? I put down my pen and closed my computer while asking God to reveal the complete truth and the accompanying balance.

I have always known in my heart of hearts that the grace of God does not give a license to acts of disobedience to His word, acts that He calls sin. Acts that much of the world no longer consider sin. Leaving the body of believers out of the discussion for a moment, let's consider the beliefs of the world at large. The world in which you and I live today has departed from any concept of absolute truth. This world, for the most part, no longer recognizes sin as sin. It has denied a moral standard; it is a world that promotes, "If it feels good, do it." For this modern world and for all intents and purposes, the concept of sin is almost foreign. A great number of people no longer even accept personal responsibility for their choices.

Many in the medical community and in educational settings, perhaps unwittingly, help to encourage the current attitudes towards accountability. It seems that, rather than hold people responsible for their heinous acts, psychiatrists and other well-educated people who are, for the most part, humanists, agnostics, or atheists call depravity, misconduct and perversions, illnesses; they find names to fit the "disease" of those gripped by tendencies toward wrongdoing. The attitude seems to be if the experts name it, they can encourage large pharmaceutical companies to search for chemicals with which to treat it. If those in the business of formulating medications can identify a drug that seems to help, they can treat the "ailment." Then, all too often, they have to search for other formulations that will treat the side effects of those drugs that were supposed to work miracles. With apologies to those who work very hard to find cures, those who are true humanitarians, I still wonder how many doctors are more interested in making money than in healing their patients. Do they have little incentive for "curing" those who continue to spend their insurance money and come up with generous "copays"?

In a similar vein, some evangelical churches and their pastors have decided to present only "positive" messages in their churches and their discipleship training. A positive message will perhaps appeal to greater numbers of people; the "positive" church may be less troubled with the possibility that their message will step on member and attendee toes and thereby cause a drop in attendance. What a disservice to our Lord and Savior who gave His life so that we could be delivered from our failings, our sicknesses, our aberrations, and our perversions. Some of these things the Bible calls sin. What a disservice to people who need to hear the truth that will set them free.

Sin. Is the body of believers known as Christians able to recognize sin today? It's definitely a controversial topic, so let's look to the Bible for a definition of sin. We learn from Scripture that Adam, the first man, disobeyed God's command not to eat of the Tree of Knowledge of Good and Evil (Genesis 3). For his disobedience, he was driven from the garden of Eden and had to earn his living by the sweat of his brow. He experienced immediate separation from God's fellowship, a separation known as spiritual death, and, eventually, physical death. In the New Testament Paul bluntly calls Adam's disobedience what it is:

> Wherefore, as by one man [Adam] *sin* entered into the world, and death by sin; and so death passed upon all men, for that all have sinned: (For until the law sin was in the world: but sin is not imputed when there is no

13

law. Nevertheless death reigned from Adam to Moses, even over them that had not sinned after the similitude of Adam's transgression . . . (Romans 5:12–14, emphasis added).

Several centuries after Adam's disobedience, King Saul of Israel disobeyed God's command to completely annihilate all the men, women, children, babies, cattle, sheep, goats, camels, and donkeys in Amalek because that nation had hindered the Israelites when they came from Egypt. No person, not even the king of Amalek, was to be spared. King Saul, chosen and anointed by God to be king of Israel, interpreted God's command to suit himself and his soldiers. He led war against the king of Amalek and his country. He killed everything but the king; his men slaughtered animals, but, with his tacit blessing, they kept the best of the animals and everything else that appealed to them. Insisting that he had fulfilled the Lord's command, Saul told the prophet Samuel that the animals his men had kept would be sacrificed to God. With a heavy heart, Samuel informed Saul that his act of disobedience was rebellion, as much a sin as witchcraft (1 Samuel 15:2–23). As a result of that act of disobedience, God even rejected Saul as king.

No, we cannot ignore God's commands just because they don't line up with the current desires and demands of a people who insist on doing life their own way. God never changes. His Word doesn't change. The only thing that should change is the methods believers and fellowships of believers commonly called churches use to present the gospel of Jesus Christ with its positive as well as its negative message. The gospel, the good news, tells you and me what Jesus did for us in an effort to bring humanity back into relationship with God. It also tells us what's wrong with our lives and how to correct what's wrong. Whether we like it or not, it is the Word of a loving God, a longsuffering God, a God who wants the world to be reconciled to Him. When we decide to participate in that reconciliation, we move into what are, for most of us, uncharted seas, and out of what is familiar and comfortable.

Life presents all of us with opportunities as well as necessities for moving out of our comfort zones. Clearly, some of us are born with passions and aspirations that keep us from settling for the status quo. Others of us go kicking and screaming as life throws us into situations we never wanted or places we never dreamed of finding ourselves. Serious chronic illness, divorce, financial loss, death of a loved one, job loss, and subsequent move to another city or state—even answering God's call to go or to do as a child of God. Any of these circumstances can thrust us into the most challenging circumstances. Our willingness to stretch and be stretched will determine how successfully we navigate those roaring tides in our lives. To paraphrase Randy Pausch (*The Last Lecture*), "We often have no choice in the hand we're dealt; we can, however, choose how we respond." It is in the response that we find our victory or our defeat.

In the following pages, I share a life that has struggled from a small town in the hills of West Virginia to a suburb of Atlanta, Georgia, and stops in between. I unveil a person who has stretched—from a timid introvert to someone who can, when necessary, talk with anyone. From an admirer of higher education to someone with a PhD. From a "Christian atheist" (Craig Groeschel says this is a person who has accepted Christ as Savior and expects to go to heaven but lives as if there is no God) to a fervent, responsive believer. From one who held on tightly to tradition and religion to a follower of Christ who has embraced His grace. My challenge to you, reader, is to examine your own dearly held beliefs and hold them up to the light of the Word of God, to follow God's path, to reprise any dreams you may have buried, to dare to stretch to the next level. As Mary Kay Ash, founder of Mary Kay cosmetics said, "*A good goal is like a strenuous exercise—it makes you stretch.*" God's goals for you are good goals.

Chapter 3

OVERCOMING THE WRONG VOICE

He that is of God heareth God's words.
–John 8:47a

———◈———

I'm Somebody. Who are you? Are you Somebody too?

Do those words sound arrogant? Self-aggrandizing?

Many of you may be remembering Emily Dickinson's poem that says just the opposite: "I'm Nobody. Who are you? Are you Nobody too?" I started to use her words. Then the brakes went on in my spirit. The Word of God proves that in God's sight you and I are not nobodies. After all, the Bible says He created humans in His image and likeness; He chose to make us like Him (Genesis 1:26). The Bible also says, ". . . we are God's [own] handiwork (His workmanship), recreated in Christ Jesus, [born anew]" (Ephesians 2:10 AMP). The key thought here is, when we come to salvation in Christ, we become somebodies. In Christ, we become sons and daughters of the Most High God (John 1:12). I choose to believe His Word about you and me, and I expand on these thoughts in a later chapter.

By the world's standards, however, I am more of the nobody that Dickinson named. Oh, a few hundred students might just remember that tough English teacher; they gave me a nickname that rhymes with Duncan. (You shouldn't have any trouble figuring that one out.) Forget that I had fewer students to fail my class each year than almost any other teacher—at least in high school. You see, as a high school and university teacher, I believed that all students, high school juniors and seniors as well as those in university, often make poor decisions. Many of them need second and third chances. I believe the Spirit of God moved on me to make them available.

God believes in multiple chances. If you don't believe it, just think of the numbers of people you know—maybe even you, yourself—who have cheated death over and over and lived to a ripe old age before giving their lives to Christ on their deathbeds.

As one who has enjoyed multiple chances myself from time to time, I believe strongly in second and third chances. I've seen them work for those who took advantage of them. I've seen that the great majority of those students who took advantage of their second and third chances proved first to themselves that they could succeed. Then they showed their parents and all the naysaying teachers who knew them as irresponsible, unmotivated, uninterested failures. Sometimes, all it took was encouragement. Sometimes, they required more than a little encouragement and patient personal coaching. At other times, they responded only to the proverbial kick in the seat of their pants, meta-phorically speaking, of course.

Besides those students, some friends, members of small groups, and other church-affiliated people, I'm just a coal miner's daughter who became the first (maybe the only) in her family, immediate and extended, to earn a PhD in anything. Consequently, a few university professors may remember me as a hard worker. Two of them may even remember they told me I was a good writer. Thankfully. Their opinion was and still is valuable to me. At the same time, that little voice between my ears reminds me that I was one English major in a cohort of about twenty-five math, science, and history majors. Nevertheless, I've always known my help comes from God.

Since elementary school, I've been writing, doing assignments. Acknowledging my need to rely on God, I prayed before and during every one of them: hundreds of papers in high school and university including a master's degree thesis, papers for presentation to scholarly conferences, a doctoral dissertation. Maybe thousands of prayers. But those assignments did not satisfy a desire to write. I'm not sure that this felt need was a "leading" from God at that time. Perhaps it was, and I just pushed it to the back as I stretched toward my own plans and goals for my life.

It could be that I still needed years of preparing and learning before I was ready to fulfill that desire. I definitely needed God's help to rise above a natural inclination toward feeling inferior to others. Anyway, I prayed over each goal and proceeded while trying to trust the Lord. Most of the time, I believed I was following His lead. In retrospect, I know that I often listened to noise, to the wrong voice: the voice of defeat, the voice of insecurity, the voice of doubt a few times. Maybe many times. I pushed toward my goals. Today, I have learned that God's thoughts for our lives are good. He orders our steps when we put our trust in Him and follow His lead. Several Scriptures declare His interest in directing our lives:

> A man's heart deviseth his way: but the LORD directeth his steps (Proverbs 16:9).

> For I know the thoughts that I think toward you, saith the LORD, thoughts of peace, and not of evil, to give you an expected end (Jeremiah 29:11).

> The steps of a good man are ordered by the LORD . . . (Psalm 37:23).

These verses sound as if God is willing to provide a GPS for us because He has a plan and a destination in mind for us.

As early as high school, I thought God might have a plan for me to write. Then, it was news articles for our high school newspaper. As a teacher I often wrote the assignments I gave my students. Later in life, I contemplated writing a novel; it just did not materialize in my head, much less on paper. Now I have no desire to write a novel or a short story. But educational writing requirements—essays, poems, short stories, research papers, master's degree thesis, dissertation—presented challenges that God helped me to conquer. They received pleasingly high marks. I even had one short story published many years ago. Not that I did it without a bit of a kick start. An editor that I knew requested that I write it. Was that God's open door to further opportunity?

Today I honestly don't know, but I prayed over the assignment and wrote a short story with a biblical Christmas theme. I thought it turned out well. I was even proud of it. Even though the editor-friend published the story without tearing it to pieces or even suggesting a single change, he never again asked me to write anything for his publication. I was just too insecure to press the point; I settled for a "safer" notoriety in my classroom. I never wrote another short story for publication.

Outside the educational and professional realms, the only other thing anyone asked me to write for publication was a Bible study on the book of Jonah for teenagers. It was an invitation that I was excited to accept, and that study, too, was published. Even though I had hopes of other invitations, no more offers or requests came from that person. So, I took stock of the lack of invitations and decided my writing must not be as strong as I had thought and secretly hoped. A good reason not to pursue writing a book! Or so my "chatterbox," that voice between my ears, told me. (Thanks to Pastor Steven Furtick for that very appropriate word.)

Maybe the reason for the lack of paid opportunities to write was my lack of faith in God and myself. Maybe it was that I tend to be lazy about some things. I've learned how difficult writing really is. Maybe it's that I continue to cling to the notion that I need inspiration to write. Forget that someone told me many years ago that writing is one-part inspiration and nine parts perspiration. In retrospect, I'm sure my major problem was the consequence of several circumstances in my life that contributed to a very hefty and unhealthy inferiority complex. And even as I write that sentence, I remember a powerful sermon on pride and its manifestation that I heard several years ago. While I remember the sermon, I can't, for the life of me, remember the minister. I just know that he dropped a bombshell in my lap when he said that an inferiority complex and shyness are evidence of pride in the life of a believer. He pointed out that these detractors indicate too much self-consciousness and not enough God-consciousness. I continue to reach for complete victory in that area.

I see now that I've indulged in self-talk, a voice that fed a feeling that I'm inadequate to the possibilities. Unwilling to stretch that far, I obviously was not ready to put my complete trust in the Lord and leave the outcome to Him. I suspect that some of you feel that way too. Do you have dreams that you have not pursued because you just don't see that you have the talent to reach the goal? How many times have you heard and maybe quoted, "I can do all things through Christ who strengthens me" (Philippians 4:13)? Are you like me, willing to believe that's true for everyone but you? I've quoted that verse time and again and reached for certain goals while slamming the door on others. I dared to believe it was true for me in some circumstances but not in others. In educational settings where I had a history of hard work and achievement, I was able to muster the courage and confidence to push forward. In other settings where the outcome was more uncertain, I was a bit more reluctant to become vulnerable to adverse criticism.

Can you see yet who had my ear? Besides my insecurities? He's the one who'll say the same kinds of things to you if you let him. He'll sit on your shoulder and whisper things like,

"Oh, you're just a nobody trying to be a somebody."

"You've screwed up your life so bad that no one will listen to you."

"You've failed at everything you've tried to do. What makes you think you'll be successful at this?"

"Okay. You have degrees. So what? So do millions of other nobodies."

"Red head, red head. Five cents a cabbage head. I'd rather be dead than red on the head."

"Those who can, DO. Those who can't, TEACH."

"You're too old to start over."

Since childhood, I've heard "Sticks and stones may break my bones, but words will never harm me." Whoever came up with that declaration was totally oblivious to the power of words to derail yourself and other people. The one who came "to steal, and to kill and to destroy" (John 10:10) knows all too well the power of words. With simple, seemingly innocent words, the serpent, also known as Satan or the devil (Revelation 12:19), approaches Eve in the Garden of Eden:

"Did God say . . . ?" Genesis 3:1

A question. No direct contradiction of God's Word at this first point of contact. Just enough of an idea to get her attention and lead her to thinking outside God's will. Just innocuous words?

According to the Bible record in Genesis 1–3, God creates the universe including the earth with all its beauties, its creeping and crawling animals, the birds of the air, and the fish and other water creatures. Then He forms Adam from the dust of the ground and breathes into him the breath of life and places him in the Garden of Eden. There Adam is surrounded with all the beauties of the earth, all kinds of pleasant looking trees with good foods that he needs to survive. There is also the Tree of Life and the Tree of Knowledge of Good and Evil. Adam can eat from all of those trees except one. About the garden, God says to Adam, "Of every tree of the garden [even the tree of life is not excluded] thou mayest freely eat: But of the tree of the knowledge of good and evil, thou shalt not eat of it: for in the day that thou eatest thereof thou shalt surely die" (Genesis 2:16b–17).

With these words, God gives Adam one rule to follow. Just one rule or law. Do not eat of the tree in the middle of the garden, the Tree of the Knowledge of Good and Evil. He gives no command to keep Adam from eating of the Tree of Life.

Knowing that Adam has no suitable companion, God puts him to sleep, takes a rib from his side, and forms woman. Adam calls her Eve. Together Adam and Eve enjoy the garden and intimate conversation with God for a period of time. Then their lives change course dramatically. Some would say the change was entirely Eve's fault.

Why do people say Eve was at fault? She pays attention to the serpent who catches her attention one day and suggests that God is withholding something good from her and Adam—that God doesn't want her to be wise. As she continues to listen to the beguiling voice, she succumbs to the idea that the forbidden fruit is beautiful to look at, good for food, and a source of wisdom. Without another thought, she eats what is forbidden. It isn't enough that she disobeys God; she also gives some of the fruit to her husband who follows her lead. His big mistake. With little or no thought for the consequences of their actions, both Eve and Adam choose not to obey God's command. The serpent wins that round! The power of his tantalizing words lead her and Adam down the path to separation from God, to misery and to physical death. What's worse, Adam's sin brings death to all humans. According to Paul, all of mankind inherits his sin: "Wherefore, as by one man [Adam] sin entered the world, and death by sin; and so death passed upon all men, for that all have sinned" (Romans 5:12).

But Jesus, the One who came to give us abundant life on this earth and in the life to come (John 10:10), knew the power of words from the beginning of time. He inspired King Solomon to warn people that "Death and life are in the power of the tongue" (Proverbs 18:21). Another translation says it this way: "The tongue [your words] can bring death or life; those who love to talk will reap the consequences" (NLT).

Even your words and mine have the power of death and life! My years of working with young people of many ages and my own experiences testify to the truth of that proverb. I've known students and adults who grew up hearing things like, "You're stupid." "I wish you had never been born." "You'll never amount to anything." Those students and adults struggled into their middle age and further, some even to their graves, believing that they could never achieve what other people around them achieved. They had financial problems. They had relationship problems. They battled to believe that God could love them. Their parents' words became a self-fulfilling prophecy. In my case, a grandparent teasingly called me "Fanny," and I thought he was emphasizing the size of my backside. Since that time, I have thought of myself as fat even when I was below the suggested normal weight for my height and age.

I have known about the power of words for many years. Still, for years I chose death. Not literal death, of course, just death to many of my aspirations and death to my belief in the talents and abilities God has given me. I listened to my own insecure inner voice that said, among other things, that I couldn't write anything that someone else had not already written better.

Then one day, something inside me convinced me to tell the story of my stretch from a beginning in a home on the other side of the tracks and a life of barely enough to a blessed life, from little education to university degrees; a stretch from insecurity to security in Christ, from fear to love; from a religion that taught me I needed to earn my way into God's favor to a relationship with that Someone I now know as the Giver of grace. Like me, many people who love God and struggle to please Him have not yet discovered what's been in Scripture all the centuries since men of God inspired by the Holy Spirit penned the words that God gave them. Their traditions and the pull of a legalistic approach to Scripture have enslaved them. Their eyes are blinded, and their traditions have become more important to them than the truth. Maybe, I reason today, I can encourage at least one reader with my story.

With a desire to help someone, even if it is just one person discover the better way, I began to write. For a while, words flowed freely. Then I began to edit. The one who came to destroy played his CD again. I was snagged. I listened. Discouragement set in, so I closed my computer for several months. I birthed nothing more until a few months ago when my pastor (Michael Turner, Turning Point Church in McDonough, Georgia) preached another of his powerful sermons. He reminded an audience of more than 500 attending that First Wednesday service that God has given to each member of his body differing talents, faculties, qualities, and functions (Romans 12: 4–6). He boldly declared that those of us who do not use our gifts and talents withhold from the world what God wants to bring to them through us.

Pastor Mike's words lit a fire under me. Could it be that I have something more to offer this world? My mind blazed with the thought that he was preaching from God-given inspiration. That inspiration was for me. Maybe for others too, but certainly for me. Unable to get away from his challenge, and, unwilling to dawdle any longer, I repented. I write.

Chapter 4

REMEMBERING MY BEGINNING

In the beginning God . . . .
–Genesis 1:1

⸺◈⸺

M ine is the story of both a physical and a spiritual journey.
It began for me in Raleigh County, West Virginia, during World
War II. Long before anyone had even dreamed of birthing suites in
fancy hospitals with Dad and relatives present, I made my appearance
in this world at Mom and Dad's three rooms and path near the banks
of New River. They told me I arrived about an hour before the doctor
got there.

As it happened, Dad and Mom lived in a coal mining "camp" in
West Virginia, a typical small community built around a company store
and a mining operation. Such a town and coal mine inspired an old
song called "Sixteen Tons," written and recorded by Merle Travis in
1946 and made popular by Tennessee Ernie Ford in the 1950s. One line
of the song says, "I owe my soul to the company store." When I asked
what that meant, Dad explained that miners could get an advance on
their meager pay between paydays to purchase necessities before the
next pay check. Miners called this advance "scrip"; it was good only at
the company store. My own dad took advantage of the opportunity for
such advances in the days when his wages were approximately $1.00
per day. So from pay period to pay period, Dad and his co-workers
owed the company store. Some people used so much scrip between
paydays that they had almost no money to supply other needs or wants.

No roads wound along the river bank into that mountain community that had formed near a coal mine and around the "company store,"
only a railroad track. People who went in and out of there had to take a

flat pump car that they had to pump or push over a mile on the rails to the nearest highway and other accoutrements of civilization. It moved by manpower. Real manpower. That August day when I was born, it was my dad's lot to muscle the pump car up the river to another town where he hoped beyond hope to find Dr. Mays, a general practitioner who made house calls. He had no phone to call the doctor and no car to drive quickly to his door. Then the two of them had to make the return trip the same way. Fortunately, he found Dr. Mays. The round trip must have seemed interminable, not only to Dad but also to my mom and waiting grandmother. He never said, but the effort he had to expend and the time it took may have given Lynn Greiner space to calm his first-time dad nerves.

Born into a family of blue-collar workers with little formal education and plenty of life smarts, I was introduced to a well-furnished bedroom of a very modest house rented from the company that owned the local coal mine. The house was a carbon copy of dozens of others situated around the company store and near the rails with their open cars that dutifully carried coal to market and returned empty to continue the process.

According to all accounts, Grandma Spencer, Mom's mother, was there with Mom—coaching, soothing, and holding Mom's hand. She was doing all the other appropriate midwife duties when I decided not to wait any longer.

As Grandma recounted the events, I came into this world with something like a misty veil over my head. Somewhat in awe, she reached out toward it. As she touched it, it evaporated. Many years later, when she thought I was old enough to hear the story, she told me she believed the veil was a sign that God had blessed me in some special way. Perhaps her remarks were inspired by a belief in old wives' fables. Perhaps the Spirit of God inspired her. From my perspective many decades later, I draw my own conclusions. I know beyond doubt that God has blessed me mightily. Indeed, I have been blessed all of my life; so has my family.

Mom, Helen Spencer Greiner, learned to trust the Lord as a child. At the age of seven she accepted Christ as her Savior. She learned to love reading the Bible early in life, and today, at age ninety-six, she still loves God's Word. Even when her parents did not go to church, she did. She lived a life of devotion to God and His church and her family. Dad came to Christ as a young man just weeks after he first saw Mom and declared that she was the woman he would marry. Shortly after they married, he was still struggling with a desire for nicotine. One day he decided to give in to the craving; he would not go on without it. His religious training taught him that to use tobacco was sin. To sin was to backslide, sometimes called "losing your salvation." To backslide was, according to the belief of the church, to separate himself from God, and that meant to him that he had to get saved all over again. So Dad, for all intents and purposes, did his best to abandon a God-first life for the next forty years.

Mom taught my sisters—eventually we became five—and me to go to church and to fear God; Dad taught us to be like Mom. We often wanted more to be like him. He wanted us to be everything she was. It was late in my life before I realized that he, in his own peculiar way, was trying to contribute to our spiritual development even though he was not walking the walk until after his first heart attack in his mid-sixties.

And so my early years helped to form who I would become as an adult. My Christian mother had a life of "dos and don'ts," many of them established as doctrines of our church and its advice to members, that guided her. Some of them reflected her own values and Dad's. She passed them on to my sisters and me. They covered many areas of our lives, and some of them were grounded in Scripture. In retrospect, I see that her rules were founded on a well-intentioned desire to help her daughters become people of character and good Christians. The church rules may have birthed from a desire of the overseers and pastors to help new converts to become Christ-like and keep the older Christians in line. The creators of what I call *Our List* did not know that some of the list would encourage us to become self-righteous people who believed we needed to earn our salvation and God's grace by our own efforts.

OUR LIST

DO—go to church every time the doors opened.

Our church encouraged regular attendance. Our Mom taught us by example and by precept. We went on Sunday morning, Sunday night, Wednesday night, and Friday night (our youth service, on the same night as all our high school football games). Nothing but sickness—Whether her own or ours—kept her kept her and us from scheduled services. This rule has proven to be a beneficial "do." It obeys God's admonition to assemble with other believers (Hebrews 10:25). We didn't like the rule, but my sisters and I learned the benefit of fellowship with like-minded people, and we made lifelong friends. Mom said we strengthened each other. Today, I find that she was right.

My sisters and I have, for the most part, practiced the rule that was Mom's and the church's.

DO—unto others as you want them to do to you (also referred to as the Golden Rule; Matthew 7:12).

DO—love your neighbor as yourself (given by Christ as the second great commandment; Matthew 22:38).

DO—share what you have with people who don't have and do good (Hebrews 13:16).

Practice the Golden Rule. Love others the way you'd like to be loved. Share what you have with others. Mom actively practiced all of that. Dad joined her in generosity. Many were the times when she gathered clothing and household goods that I thought our family really needed to pass on to those who, for one reason or another, had far less than we had or nothing more than the clothes on their backs. I remember we gave sacrificially to some whose home had burned. Others simply had fallen on bad times and had pawned or sold anything with value in their house just to survive.

Somehow we never missed what we gave. If we had a clean dress for school each day, a nicer outfit for Sunday, and shoes to wear, we counted ourselves blessed. With her example and Dad's deference to Mom, our parents trained us that we could always trust God to provide enough for ourselves with some left over for others. They were practicing what the writer of Hebrews urges: "But to do good and to communicate forget not: for with such sacrifices God is well pleased" (Hebrews 13:16). Another version of Scripture says it this way: "Do not forget to do good and to share with others, for with such sacrifices God is pleased" (NIV).

Obviously, Mom reached into the Scripture for her practice of giving. She knew what Paul wrote to the church at Corinth:

> But this I say, He which soweth sparingly shall reap also sparingly; and he which soweth bountifully shall reap also bountifully. Every man according as he purposeth in his heart, so let him give; not grudgingly, or of necessity: for God loveth a cheerful giver. And God is able to make all grace abound toward you; that ye, always having all sufficiency in all things, may abound to every good work. (2 Corinthians 9:6–8)

The New Living Translation says it this way:

> Remember this—a farmer who plants only a few seeds will get a small crop. But the one who plants generously will get a generous crop. You must each decide in your heart how much to give. And don't give reluctantly or in response to pressure. "For God loves a person who gives cheerfully." And God will generously provide all you need. Then you will always have everything you need and plenty left over to share with others.

I like another translation of 2 Corinthians 9:8 I found on a greeting card: "God can bless you with *everything* you need, and you will always have *more* than enough to do all kinds of good things for others" (CEV, emphasis added). That worked for my family and others we knew. We gave as unto God. We tested Him. We proved Him. We learned that you cannot outgive Him. I remember that God Himself, through the prophet Malachi, invited the people of Israel to prove Him and learn for themselves that He would bless them so bountifully that they would not be able to receive all of his blessing. He also promised to keep the fruit from falling off the vine before it ripens and to "rebuke the devourer," the insects and plagues, so that they couldn't destroy the livelihood of His people (Malachi 3:10–11).

Although the Holy Spirit directed Malachi's words to the people of Israel, those words also apply to the followers of Christ today. Scripture tells us if we are Christ's, then we are the seed of Abraham and heirs, along with the father of faith, of the promises of God (Galatians 3:29).

Indeed, we can, by faith, receive that promised blessing and have enough for ourselves and some left over for others. Or vice versa. Enough for others and plenty left over for ourselves. My sisters and I saw it happen again and again.

One time when I was about four years old, my family stuffed Dad's sister and her four children along with our grandfather and Mom, Dad, and three children into our almost "new" but still small home—the one I grew up in. This one was four rooms and a path to an outdoor toilet. Aunt Dora's husband was in the US Navy at the time, and she needed a temporary home until they could relocate. Four adults and seven children squeezed into our four-room house with two bedrooms. How did we ever do it?

I really don't know for sure, but I don't think that we children ever realized how crowded we were. I only remember that I didn't feel deprived until one of my cousins was diagnosed with scarlet fever and had to be quarantined. The Greiner girls were packed off to Grandma Spencer's house for the duration. Except for that time, our nights were like camping out as we made sleeping pallets on the floors and made up the living room sofa for the grandfather whom we called Poppy Brick. And Mom says it helped that Grandma Spencer invited the Greiner girls to spend some time with her and Poppy George.

Close communion? By all means. A far different life from that which many families in the US experience today. Now even parents of modest means want every child to have a separate bedroom with closets full of clothes and boxes, baskets and shelves loaded with toys, and electronic devices to occupy their time and attention. Conversations and family relationships are fractured at best today; at worst they are nonexistent. Maybe it has something to do with living in too much space instead of too little.

> **DO**—tithe on every bit of income that comes to you and support foreign missions.

Mom understood and taught us that a tithe is 10 percent. If she gave back to God by taking ten percent of her income to the church where she was a member, she believed she was fulfilling God's desire for her and setting herself up to receive His promise for her obedience. For Mom, a stay-at-home mother and homemaker, her only income was the living allowance Dad (who didn't tithe at this time) gave her to pay the household bills, buy our clothing, and feed the mouths—not only of our family but also of the visiting family members and ministers who came regularly on Sundays after preaching their lengthy sermons at our church. That's all the money she had at her disposal. So she tithed on it, and God blessed the remaining 90 percent to cover our needs. She took God at His command to bring all the tithe into the storehouse (the local church) and received His promise of blessing (Malachi 3:10–11). Tithing and giving was one "Do" that all of us sisters eventually learned well, but we learned it in incremental steps.

One time, when I was about eleven years old, Mom's tithing was put to the acid test. For some reason Dad was out of work and couldn't find a job. He had friends who had heard that the auto industry was booming in Cleveland, Ohio, so he packed his clothes and left for Cleveland with Mom's blessing. Almost immediately, he went to work with General Motors and had a reasonably good income. However, he had to have a place to stay and food to eat in Cleveland and still find money to keep up the home in West Virginia and put fuel in the car that would inevitably make weekend trips back home. Rentals were expensive there and almost impossible to find. After a month or two of living apart from the love of her life and dealing with the issues of daily living, Mom left us kids with Grandma and went to Cleveland to look for a place for everyone to live.

Days of searching yielded no results. People either did not want to rent to families with children or the apartment or house was far too small or the rent was too expensive for my parents. Winter and its woes took over; Dad was still there. We were still in West Virginia where we had graduated to a beautiful house with two bedrooms, a living room with a fireplace that heated the whole house, and an eat in kitchen. Not to forget the "path." Because of the double living expenses, those of us at home found ourselves stretching what we had to eat. Many days it was biscuits and water gravy for breakfast and sandwiches made of biscuits and government-issued cheese for lunch. We thanked God for Poppy Brick's disability benefits; his emphysema (I think we call it COPD today) kept him disabled and unable to work. But, his lack of sufficient income to support himself qualified him for government "commodities." Every month we looked forward to the day when he brought home delicious cheese in a five-pound block, dried eggs, flour, and peanut butter; sometimes, he received canned beef or pork which complemented the canned vegetables and fruit Mom always worked hard to preserve in the summer.

It was during this time that Dad was in one state and we were in another that Mom's resolve to tithe was put to a strong test. While Dad's earnings were good, he was not earning enough money to support two households completely. Christmas was coming, and Mom calculated she did not have even enough money to buy food and pay winter utility bills—much less Christmas gifts for the family. Without a word to anyone, she kept her tithe to use for necessities. Soon after that she told us girls the circumstances after her decision. She confessed that the month she did not give her tithe into the church, one of us became ill and had to see a doctor. His bill was the exact dollar amount of the tithe. She declared that she had learned her lesson. I learned from her.

No, I did not learn, I do not believe, and I'm not saying that God made one of her children sick to punish Mom for not tithing that month even though it may have seemed that way to her. On the contrary, God does not bring sickness and disease; He made provision through Jesus Christ for healing and wellness (1 Peter 2:24; Psalm 107:20). Our heavenly Father loves and disciplines His children (Hebrews 12:5–11), but nowhere does the Bible say that He disciplines us by causing us or someone we love to become sick or to die or by bringing disaster on us. It was only under the Old Covenant that sickness and disease were part of the curse of the law (Deuteronomy 28:20–22, 27, 35, 58–61). Paul declared that "Christ has redeemed us" from that curse (Galatians 3:13).

After that incident, winter was in full swing, and Christmas was right around the corner. In spite of the shortage of funds, Mom and Dad found a way to give us one sled to share for Christmas. We also got our precious brown bags of fruit and nuts and candy: one apple, one orange, a few nuts to crack, and some hard candy per child. Nothing ever tasted as good as those Christmas brown-bag treats. We ate scant meals. We cut wood to burn in the fireplace and in the kitchen cook stove. We wore a sweater in the house when it was too cold. We carried our biscuit and cheese sandwiches to school for lunch. We survived. Like the foolish child I was, I blessed the day when we could afford to buy white loaf bread with its neatly and uniformly cut slices and make sandwiches. I thought I had died and gone to heaven. Now my sandwiches looked like those of my classmates. No longer did I have to suffer lunches that advertised our poverty.

From Mom we learned not only to tithe but also to give offerings, especially to support missionaries and their work in foreign countries. Though she ventured only once to another country, foreign missions were one of Mom's passions. She gave sacrificially to support the spread of the good news of Christ. She inspired her daughters to do as she did.

The only time Mom left the US, she was in her early eighties. She went on her first and only cruise to the Bahamas with my husband and me. She told the rest of the family that she was going on a mission trip even though we had no planned ministry activities. The first day in Nassau, we went to a shopping area near the port. Before we left the straw market, Mom went to a rest room where she found a single Bahamian woman whose duty was to keep the restroom clean and supplied with all things the visitors would need. Without hesitation, Mom engaged this woman in conversation. It turned out that she had been a Christian but was not living a God-first life; she wanted to "come back to the Lord." So Mom promptly prayed for her and with her as she rededicated her life to the Lord. In her mind, my mother had fulfilled her mission. She left Nassau happy and at peace with God.

My baby sister and I have been able to do what she could not. With my husband, I have ministered in Mexico and Peru; Kathy and her husband ministered in Ukraine. All of us joined Mom in extensive and selfless ministry in our various communities. A granddaughter loves the Jewish people and has traveled to Israel; she has been involved in missions in Mexico, and she and her daughter had their first mission trip together to Mexico in recent months.

Both Mom and Dad taught the principles of giving and generosity by example. They never turned away anyone who came to their house hungry. If the people looked unkempt, they often invited them to sit on the front porch steps rather than in our kitchen to eat, but they ate. Sometimes they didn't need the hot meal; sometimes they just needed something with which to feed their family. Those people went home with a variety of canned goods in the winter months and fresh vegetables from our garden in the summer. The house I grew up in always had enough to keep us alive and, most often, we had enough left to help someone else.

DO keep your word to other people and don't lie. God doesn't like liars; He promises they won't go to heaven (Revelation 21:27).

Over the years, I have had a difficult time with that one. Not with doing what I said I would do. That has been no problem. It's the latter part of that teaching that I checked off, secure for the longest time that I was doing what was right. The Holy Spirit has helped to keep me straight when I paid attention to him, but for a long time I felt no compunction for withholding part of the truth and allowing people to believe a lie. Occasionally, I exaggerated to present myself in a better light. Over and over again, I found myself asking God to forgive me.

Earlier in life, like many other people, I reasoned that it was better to tell "a little white lie" (a Satanic invention; a lie is a lie) or to skirt the truth than to hurt someone's feelings. If my friend asked me to approve her new sweater, I could not tell her it was hideous, could I, even if I thought so? I tried first just complementing the color or style. I tried other evasive practices. Finally, I learned that good friends appreciate knowing that they can depend on me to be honest and not to ask my opinion if they don't want an honest answer. But I've also learned that honesty doesn't have to be harsh. It can and should be couched in courtesy and grace.

DO — be on time to appointments.

Oh, how hard that last one has been for me. I'm still time-challenged. For Mom, being on time meant arriving twenty to thirty minutes early. Not me! You'd think that I'm not my mother's child. Even today. Now don't get me wrong. I love being on time and have learned the value of that discipline in my profession and in my work for God. However, I think being on time means showing up for the appointment or church service on the dot, certainly not much more than ten minutes early. My natural bent could easily be persuaded to think like a friend of ours from New York. She shared that for her and her friends in New York being on time meant arriving twenty to thirty minutes after the appointed hour. She declared they would have been appalled to have guests invited for dinner at 7 P.M. show up before 7:20. If that's truly a New York attitude (and I'm not convinced that it is), I think I'd find my place there very quickly.

It seems that a number of my church family must be from New York (Forgive me, New Yorkers). Sometimes at the starting time only half of the seats are filled. When we were in our older and smaller auditorium, by ten minutes into the service we found ourselves filling the auditorium and sometimes spilling into the overflow. Today, in a larger auditorium, the practice of some is the same. Ten or fifteen minutes after service begins, people are still coming in. Recent visits to other churches uncover the same tendencies. But I hasten to defend the latecomers; at least they don't let being late hinder their desire and willingness to be in church.

Thankfully, most churches of any size seem to have abandoned the practice of my childhood church. While I was growing up and even later, more often than not, the officiating minister delayed the start of the service waiting for more of the members or visitors to show up. He or she seemed to think that it was not worth the effort to begin a service if the song leader (the precursor to the worship leader) was late or if only three or four were present. Many years ago—I may have still been a teenager—I decided to count how many precious minutes were lost because church did not start on time. I reasoned that if four people wait for six or eight minutes, that's close to a half hour lost. If four hundred people experienced the same kind of delay, many would shrug off the loss of time. They would never say that's more than four hundred minutes lost. My young mind did.

Today, I appreciate so much that my church starts precisely on time. People's time is precious. Not to start on time speaks loudly to those there that their time means nothing. It could seem to them that they are penalized for being present on time.

The "Don'ts" added to biblical mandates and personal choices were numerous, but my sisters and I learned them and kept them under the threat of dire punishment. Most of the time. Well, truth be told, *some* of the time.

OUR DON'T LIST

DON'T smoke or drink alcoholic beverages or chew (tobacco) or run around with those who do.

Chewing gum was okay except in church. Use of tobacco, recreational drugs (illegal then and still today in most states), and alcoholic beverages was said to be a sin. Besides that, our religious training said these substances lead to bondage and addictions. Today, I know for sure that they can lead to bondage and addictions. It's rare to find a family today that doesn't have at least one family member who's in bondage to one substance or another. Statistics released by the Pew Research Center in 2017 found that almost half the American adult population of the US had a friend or family member involved in substance abuse.

I decided early in life that, even if I had had the sanction of the church (and I did not) to have a glass of wine or other alcoholic beverage with a meal, I would not. My decision grew out of what I had witnessed and personal taste. I had seen many drunkards in my young life. I didn't like their behaviors when they were under the influence. Some of them became violent; others of them became weepy and self-pitying. Also, since I seemed to have a penchant for, possibly even an addiction to, chocolate and sugar, I decided not to begin something else I might like too much. I also reasoned that it was foolish anyway to develop a taste for a beverage that smelled horrible and tasted, in most cases, like vinegar. To me, at least.

DON'T dance.

Our church and our grandmother-pastor declared dancing to be "worldly"; they said it was "of the devil." They said it can get you in trouble with the opposite sex, especially if you dance too close. While I can admit some validity to the reasoning, with this "rule," an enjoyable form of exercise was denied to us.

Oh, I wanted to dance. My sisters did too. Mom allowed us to watch *American Bandstand* on TV and listen to the music. I admired the pretty girls on the show who danced so well, who seemed completely unselfconscious. Two of my sisters watched, practiced, and learned to dance. I was afraid to. I wanted to dance, but I didn't want to sin. And I didn't want to disappoint my mom and dad. Even after I read in the Bible that King David of Israel danced before the Lord with all his might, I could do no more than raise my hands in worship or clap them in appreciation and tap my foot when I really wanted to dance before the Lord with abandon like King David. So I finally determined that if I danced, it would be under the power of the Holy Spirit as I worshipped in spirit and in truth. That was an approved behavior. It would not lead to "unseemly" conduct.

Many years later, when worship music at church or at home draws me to worship, I'm able to lose some of the self-consciousness and the care for what others think. I can dance before the Lord when it's just him and me. That's not a problem. I've learned it's liberating to worship the Lord in dance—at home. A few times I've even tried moving with the music in churches where the practice was encouraged. Even though the psalmist declared that people should worship with all kinds of instruments, hand clapping, and dancing (Psalm 150:14a), my religious training has made me uncomfortable with dancing in a public worship. I tried it only a few times.

While a growing number of pastors and worship leaders promote a choreographed dance in worship, the jury is still out for me on that practice. My major concern is that such a dance inspires spectating and not participating in recognizing and honoring the true "worth-ship" of the Father in heaven. Jesus said there would come a time when true worshipers must and would worship the Father in spirit and truth (John 4:24–25). So if I dance in the spirit in my worship of the Lord, I am refreshed. I encourage that practice. On the other hand, I acknowledge that worship looks different to different people and that it's not my place to judge another man's servant (Romans 14:4).

Our true worship depends a great deal on empowerment by the Holy Spirit once we have made Jesus the Lord of our lives. Coming to Christ in faith and accepting Him as Lord and Savior assures that our spirit is one with His. As John Piper has said, "True worship comes only from spirits made alive and sensitive by the quickening of the Spirit of God" (*Desiring God*). To worship Him in spirit involves focus on Him and His works; it involves grateful regenerated hearts and emotions; it involves full participation in the worship experience without regard for the comfort and beauty (or lack thereof) of our surroundings, what the worship band is doing or not doing, or what the people surrounding us are or are not doing. True worship is a personal thing, an attitude of the heart, and it revitalizes and energizes those who worship.

DON'T go to the movies and other "worldly" entertainment.

Grandma and other ministers in the church leadership declared that movies are of the devil, that they'll pollute your mind. According to them, the theater is the devil's playground—just like the dance floor and the skating rink.

Grandma had a valid point; it's pretty good advice much of the time especially considering today's PG-13 and R-rated offerings. My husband and I have walked out of a few PG-13 movies because of the content, especially the fairly explicit sexual activity that leaves little to the imagination. Walking out became easier after the first time, but we kept losing the price of the ticket—not a small sum of money. If it ever happens again, I'll ask to be reimbursed or try to schedule a different movie. It can't hurt to try.

The Spirit of God is a good guide. I've found that it pays to listen to the Holy Spirit when He nudges me in regard to my choice of entertainment, whether it's music or movies or television shows or something else. Often, I'm reminded of something Pastor Andy Stanley said in a televised sermon many years ago. He said it always amazed him that Christians would pay their hard-earned money to see movies promoting activities that they would have to ask God to forgive them for. I have to agree with him. His words have provided a standard for me many times.

DON'T go "too far" with your date.

Unfortunately, "too far" was never quite defined, but, as I look back, the implication was, "Girls, guard yourselves. Don't get involved in petting and, especially, don't get pregnant before marriage. That would be a sin as well as a disgrace for you and for your family." Christian girls were not just encouraged; they were mandated to practice abstinence in spirit as well as body.

No one ever said anything about the role of the boys in getting the girls pregnant and that they, too, should practice abstinence until after marriage. Maybe that's because I was part of a family of girls, and the church I attended had a female pastor and only one or two teenaged boys. Thankfully, many pastors today have the fortitude and the love for young people to encourage all young people—boys as well as girls—to live according to biblical principles and save their intimate relationships for marriage.

Such teaching, backed by the Word of God, would have been appropriate in my adolescence even though parents and pastors were reluctant to speak of sexual matters from the pulpit. Paul warns Christians to "Flee fornication" (1 Corinthians 6:18); to put it another way, the Amplified Bible says, "Run away from sexual immorality [in any form, whether thought or behavior, whether visual or written]. . . the one who is sexually immoral sins against his own body." The Merriam-Webster dictionary defines *fornication* as "consensual sexual intercourse between two persons not married to each other." Did the young hear the biblical teaching in my youth? Do they hear it now? We don't have to look very far to find the answer to those questions. The rising birth rate among unmarried girls and women—in the church or not—testifies to the lack of teaching or the lack of hearing what the Bible has always taught.

Even the church has its share of unwed parents. Perhaps the unwillingness of the world to subscribe to a set of moral standards has infiltrated the Body of Christ. Several statistics testify to the loosening or lack of biblical standards among younger people today. For example, the number of professing Christians who think there's nothing wrong with couples living together in sexual intimacy before they get married has grown to an astounding number. George Barna, a well-known pollster, surveyed evangelical Christians a few years ago. From that survey came very disturbing statistics. He reported that 39 percent reported that they believe it's "morally acceptable for couples to live together before marriage"; that same survey also found that one out of three "born-again Christians," those who reported having received Christ as their Savior and Lord and were expecting to make heaven their final destination, accept same-sex unions. (*World,* 12/06/03, p. 33).

It appears that more and more people think the Bible should evolve to meet the standards they now tolerate as morally acceptable. The statistics reveal a definite reluctance—even among Christians—to use the Bible as a moral standard today. Apparently, no one is immune to the desire to "have it my way" even when that way is in direct opposition to God's Word.

DON'T even think of getting married again if you're divorced.

Our church preached strongly that if you divorce and remarry, you're living in adultery. Therefore, you can't be a member of the church, and you won't go to heaven unless your first spouse is already dead. Even those who had divorced and married someone else before they gave their hearts to God and trusted Christ as their Savior were not eligible for church membership. The position of the church baffled me. Not one time did I hear Scriptures or explanations of what makes adultery an unforgiveable sin, a sin worse than lying or gluttony or malice or other forms of disobedience. The pastors and overseers also failed to point out that Jesus opposed divorce but allowed for those whose spouses were unfaithful to get a divorce (Matthew 5:31–32). They ignored that He also simply directed the woman caught in the act of adultery to go and sin no more. He didn't rain fire from heaven down upon her. He didn't tell her she was bound for hell. He didn't even ban her from His presence.

> **DON'T** swim with the opposite sex (except for family members) and stay away from skating rinks.

Our church hierarchy said that swimming with the opposite sex who were not family members would put undue pressure on young people's raging hormones. And it obviously can. Skating rinks, as those concerned with our eternal salvation pointed out, were places where an abundance of immoral activity often occurs — activities such as drunkenness, sexual intercourse, perverse behaviors, and drug sales and use. That was true then; it is still true today. Unfortunately, leaders and parents just handed out the rules; they did not teach young people how and why to live pure and holy lives without legislation.

> **Don't** gamble or play games with cards or dice that are used for gambling.

Abstaining from gambling did not pose a problem for me. I saw too many families whose lives were in shambles because one or more of their parents gambled away their livelihood. But playing cards and using dice in games that did not involve gambling? For years, I tried to get an understanding of the reason for forbidding the use of cards and dice in games. The only answer I could get was that people might think you're gambling, and gambling was wrong. Thankfully, I didn't have to ask what was wrong with gambling. Like so many other children and adults, I accepted the rule without lots of questions. Today, I think this "advice" was given that we might steer clear of becoming addicted to gambling and that we could avoid even the appearance of evil.

Don't wear clothing that is typical of the opposite sex.

This rule was for the benefit of both men and women. It was based on an Old Testament admonition that men and women should not wear each other's clothing (Deuteronomy 22:5). It ignored the jeans and slacks made specifically for women. It ignored the historical fact that men living when that law was given wore robes very similar in make to those which women wore. So jeans, slacks, and shorts were, for a long time, not part of my wardrobe for school or for recreation outside my own yard. Heaven help me when I played volleyball with the team at school. More often than not, the movements in the game caused a skirt to reveal so much skin that Mom finally relented and allowed her daughters to wear blue jeans just for sports. This allowance opened the door to questions about why we didn't "break" other rules. Some of us did.

Women, don't paint your faces (wear makeup) or dye your hair.

The explanation to this rule was something like this: "You'll look like Jezebel, and you know what happened to her. She fell off a balcony, killed herself, and the dogs ate her up." After a bit of questioning, I learned more of the story. The Bible account says Jezebel painted her face and put on her royal garments when it appeared that she might be in line for execution by Jehu, newly anointed king of Israel. At the king's command, her servants threw her off her balcony; dogs ate her body, except for her skull, her feet and the palms of her hands, just as the prophet Elijah had prophesied years before (2 Kings 9:30–35). And as for coloring your hair, that, too, was taboo. The explanation was that if God had wanted your hair to be a different color, He would have given you a different color. Those in leadership over us in the Lord said that the same or a similar fate to that of Jezebel could await those who wore makeup and dyed their hair. As a teenager, I wanted to obey the rule, but I also wanted to look as good as my friends who wore makeup. From time to time, I wore lipstick at school and scrubbed it off before leaving for home. Imagine my consternation the day I forgot to remove it and faced my shocked mother with red lips.

Possibly more than one person has been hindered spiritually by an uneven application of these rules. In some cases, a pastor would tell a member of his or her congregation that bleached blonde hair or dyed hair was a sign of hidden sin in the life of the individual. Then, when that individual went to a district or state or international meeting of like churches, there were sometimes representatives of the hierarchy who had disregarded the rules—and they were sitting on the stage in full view of all.

Don't wear jewelry.

In an attempt to stay true to the warning of Peter and Timothy that women should not depend on jewelry and other outward adornment for their beauty (1 Peter 3:3 and 1 Timothy 2:9), our pastors and leaders took these verses out of context and took a stand. It seems that to be "safe," women should not use any makeup or wear any jewelry. To add evidence for their position, they frequently read Isaiah's warning that God would punish the daughters of Zion for their haughtiness and their "wanton eyes," that He would take away all their jewelry, their changes of clothing, and their hair products and leave them with clothing made of sackcloth and "burning instead of beauty" (Isaiah 3:16–24). As I think back on my life, I can't remember that our ministers and leaders ever said anything about changes of clothing from the pulpit—even though they did occasionally preach that women should not wear short hair or style their hair in rolls around the backs of their heads with a "hair rat."

No jewelry? Those of us with an inclination to think for ourselves found a contradiction in the teaching and the practice. *No* jewelry. It seemed as if that rule should apply to both men and women. However, the men and some of the women, including my very strict grandmother, obviously did not. For some reason, watches, watch chains, and men's cuff links and tie clasps eventually were overlooked under this rule, but even simple wedding rings were not allowed. At some point in my early life, women, including female evangelists, began to wear cuff links and broaches, some of them large and showy. My youthful mind asked, "Isn't that jewelry too?"

No makeup? Well, that was also problematic. We children watched as mothers and grandmothers powdered their faces. Wasn't that makeup? Some even wore foundation, but none ever dared color their eyebrows, their cheeks, their eyelashes, or their lips. The one time I ever knew my mother to put on any kind of makeup, she had gone to a home cosmetics show and sale. All the women there knew she didn't wear makeup, so they persuaded her to act as the model. She came home looking glamorous to our childish eyes. To Dad, she looked like something else. He "suggested" in very authoritative tones that she go and wash that junk off her face. No satisfying answer about the discrepancies in the teachings and the practices surfaced. I learned early in life not to ask aloud too many questions that would seem to challenge what the church taught.

And the list went on. After much soul searching and trying to sort out the reasons behind the list, I truly believe today that the intent of it was not to harm or to put unnecessary restrictions on Christians. Coming from a loving church hierarchy and loving parents, the rules and regulations were sometimes based on Scripture taken out of context, but all were meant to help children to develop character and believers of all ages to live up to a perceived standard of holiness. The *Dos* and *Don'ts* were designed to help us become people of integrity and character and to keep us safe from the contamination of the world. It was important to our parents and grandparents and spiritual leaders that we "abstain from all appearance of evil" (1 Thessalonians 5:22). Many, many years later, when different members of the church hierarchy and a veritable multitude of counselors realized they had taken a stand on misunderstandings of Scripture, died-in-the-wool "believers" maintained their grip on tradition and dogma. Inevitable splits divided friends and family members as dissenting groups clung—and still cling—to the old interpretation of Scripture.

In retrospect, it seems that my family and other well-meaning people who loved the Lord tried to legislate salvation and holiness. It worked for me; I was afraid of God, and I was determined to do whatever they said to do if it would help me to avoid hell. The bad thing about my fearful life is that I found myself living without what A.W. Tozer calls a "holy desire." I just couldn't have a close relationship with someone whom I feared so much.

What I didn't know for too many years is that such "guidelines" foster a mindset, a "religion," rather than a relationship with our Savior.

The rules encouraged me to work harder and do more to earn my salvation. They encouraged self-righteousness as I checked off the Dos and Don'ts and compared myself to the lists and to others. Pride in my ability to keep the rules emerged. Taught to embrace such a line of thinking, I believed that my salvation depended on me, not on the Christ who gave His life to satisfy the sin debt of every person who ever lived—past, present, and future. Eventually, I realized my faith was in my ability to keep the checklist. It was not in God. I was into my fourth decade before I began to understand that it is not possible for humans to please God by keeping "the law," not the Old Testament Law nor the laws of organizations, no matter how sincere and pious these groups are.

Now, I'll be quick to admit that sometimes God deals with individuals to "give up" certain things, things that never bother other individuals. Take my grandmother-pastor, for instance. She shared that when she started preaching she loved her coffee and drank pots of it every day. If she didn't have it, she became irritable and searched for something to satisfy her need. One day as she was in prayer, God spoke to her spirit that she was addicted to coffee; she should give it up. She did. But not once did she preach or teach or advise other people to give up their coffee. She knew that God had spoken to her individually. It was not a requirement to be taught to others.

Many years ago, I experienced something similar. My "addiction" was to chocolate. I must have loved it from the day I was born. My dad loved it, so my mom made large skillets of fudge at least once a week. We ate gallons of chocolate ice cream. In winter, we guzzled hot cocoa at our house. So, as an adult, I often found myself craving chocolate. If there wasn't any in the house, I ate practically everything in sight trying to find something that would stop the craving. I recognized that I was hooked, but still, I didn't give it up. That was not to happen until I decided to fast a food I loved to get God to do something for me. (I wrongly believed that an individual could "move" God to action by making a deal with Him.) After considering my addiction, I gave up chocolate. Thinking that I needed to make a vow to God, I promised to give it up for the rest of my life if He would save my dad. The only time I consumed it for the next twenty years or more was by mistake. Once or twice in the last few years, I have eaten a sliver to show appreciation to someone who had made a special chocolate dessert for me or our small group. But each time, I have felt the weight of my unnecessary promise to God.

My point is simple. The Spirit of God often nudges individuals to do or not do things about which He says nothing to the collective body of believers. Today, I can be in a group eating chocolate candies, chocolate cake to die for, chocolate pie—all things chocolate. Am I required to have nothing to do with those who indulge and have more power to stop or to moderate than I do? Of course not! If I am sitting down to a meal that provides something I should not eat for the sake of my health, should I impolitely decline to eat at the same table with those who can eat it? I wouldn't think of doing such a thing; would you? Do I refuse to eat at restaurants with bars just because I've decided to be a teetotaler? Of course not. Now, if I were a recovering alcoholic, I would have every reason to want to be as far from the bar as possible. But I've never been addicted to intoxicating beverages—I don't even like them—so it's not a problem for me. Yet, Christians often find themselves gagging at similar gnats and swallowing camels.

Perhaps God has spoken to your spirit about something else—not to buy that new car that you want so dearly because your budget can't handle it just now; to give someone else money for their needs when you had been saving for months just to be able to afford what you thought you needed; to empty your savings account to support ministry somewhere; to visit someone in the hospital or nursing home; to invite someone to eat with you; to read and study only from a specific translation of the Bible. One of the things I think we all have to do is to listen as the still, small voice of the Holy Spirit speaks to us and challenges us in certain areas and not, then, to try to apply that requirement or direction to the lives of everyone else.

Jesus came to this earth to find and save the lost (Luke 19:10). He wants His followers to go into all the world and preach the gospel to everyone (Mark 16:15), not to go and make clones of themselves.

Chapter 5

DISCOVERING A DIFFERENT GIFT

For by grace are ye saved through faith . . .
it is the gift of God.
–Ephesians 2:8

C hristmas Day was crawling towards us. When Christmas Eve finally arrived, Mom sent three reluctant and emotionally "wired" sisters to their beds early "so Santa can come." The three of us shared a small room with a full-sized bed. Eventually, after several warnings from our mom and dad in the kitchen, the giggling and whispering stopped. Finally, the steady quiet breathing of my younger sisters signaled that they had not had the same trouble I was having going to sleep. Excitement and anticipation danced around in my belly. Christmas tree lights casting a soft glow in the living room invaded our doorless bedroom and mesmerized me. The colored lights sparkling in the dark room transformed our small living room into a magical place where any child's dream could come true, even mine.

Suddenly I heard a knock at the back door and a somewhat muffled "Ho, ho, ho!" Sucking in my breath, I ignored the less baritone and more soprano tones of that wished-for greeting. The figure formed around the words—not their tones. Surely, it was the little old man with a belly like a bowl full of jelly.

Slowly and quietly I let out my breath, trying not to make a sound. My next thought was to awaken my sisters so they could hear that Santa had made it to our house. But, almost immediately, I wondered why he had knocked. He was supposed to slide down the chimney. What was he doing coming through the door and the back door at that? If he was coming through the door, why wasn't he at the front door right there beside the Christmas tree that filled the room with promises of something good to come? Was the coveted doll in his sack? I decided to let Redith and Carol sleep.

Thinking of that night so long ago, I remember a different kind of gift—the gift that God so freely gave. According to Scripture, God so loved the world that He *gave*—He gave me and everyone else in this world—a free gift. That gift was His only begotten Son, destined to die a sinner's death that the world might be saved. That gift extends to whoever can believe in Him (John 3:16). With His death and resurrection, Jesus made available the gift that cannot be earned. No one can ever deserve it. It is God's gift to all mankind, to *all* who will receive it by faith. It is His grace, His unmerited favor, that provided then, and still makes available today, deliverance from the bondage of sin and provision for all the needs of life—spiritual, physical, mental and emotional, and financial. It is the gift the Apostle Paul described when he wrote, "For by grace are you saved through faith: it is the gift of God" (Ephesians 2:8).

How do we access these promised provisions? By faith. The same faith, the same complete reliance on and trust in God that opens the door to eternal salvation also opens the door to our Father's other provisions. By faith we choose to receive what He makes available. Or we can turn our backs on His gift. Or we can get lost in the misunderstanding that we have to work to please God. Or we can choose to believe that it's all up to God, that He'll do what He wants to do no matter what we do because He's in control. Where do we get the belief that God is in control of everything?

Try as I may, I can't find a firm foundation in Scripture for this interpretation. Many Bible scholars, people who have earned doctorates from seminaries, disagree with my understanding; they promote the idea that God's sovereignty puts Him in control of everything. I believe semantics is a source of confusion and disagreement. A great many people see no difference between the terms "sovereign" and "in control." There is a difference. God is, beyond all doubt, sovereign. He is the King of kings and the Lord of lords. He is matchless; He is independent, absolute, and superior. He is supreme. Above Him there is no other. The Bible says He is "Alpha and Omega, the beginning and the end" (Revelation 21:6). It also says that

Christ is the visible image of the invisible God. He existed before anything was created and *is supreme* over all creation, for through him God created everything in the heavenly realms and on earth. He made the things we can see and the things we can't see . . . Everything was created through him and for him. He existed before anything else, and he holds all creation together. (Colossians 1:15–17 NLT, emphasis added)

God has the power and the authority do anything. He can direct or change the course of events and people's lives, but He will never force himself and His desires on anyone. I propose that He is not "in control" of everything. He doesn't control our choices, for example. He gave Adam and Eve the power of choice. He gives people today the same power. He does not force people to accept His gift of eternal life. He does not "send" people to hell. He is the great healer, the giver of life, the provider, the epitome of love, the deliverer. He will also, one day, be the great judge (Revelation 20:11–12).

To say that "God is in control" suggests that He is the one who makes everything happen. The very idea should raise questions for everyone. Was God in control when Hitler and His followers exterminated millions of Jews? Was God in control when the little baby was born with no arms and legs? Was He in control when the high school graduates celebrated by getting drunk, wrapped their car around a telephone pole, and died in the accident? Was He in control when the abusive father beat his wife to death in front of his children? Was He in control as the mother's boyfriend tortured the eight-month-old baby to death? Is He in control when we eat and drink ourselves into obesity and its accompanying diseases? Did He not give to human beings the privilege and the ability to choose, even to make choices that would keep them out of heaven?

The Bible does indeed support God's sovereignty, His supreme and ultimate power. I wholeheartedly accept and believe that God is supreme. There is no greater power than His. However, I also see that, according to Scripture, He gave some of His power and authority to mankind when He gave Adam and Eve dominion over the earth. He said, on the sixth day of Creation,

"Let Us (Father, Son, Holy Spirit) make man in Our image, according to Our likeness, [not physical, but a spiritual personality and moral likeness]; and let them have complete authority over the fish of the sea, the birds of the air, the cattle, and over the *entire* earth, and over everything that creeps and crawls on the earth." (Genesis 1:26 AMP, emphasis added)

God gave the humans He created control over everything on earth. Then, Adam's disobedience in the garden of Eden produced a horrendous effect on the earth. When he chose to disobey God, Adam relinquished the dominion over the earth that God had given him to Satan.

Scripture reveals this turnover of power again during Christ's temptation in the wilderness. When the Spirit led Jesus into the wilderness to be tempted, the Bible says that, in one instance, Satan showed Jesus all the kingdoms of the world and promised, "I'll give you all these that have been handed to me if You will fall down and worship me because they're in my power to give" (Luke 4:5–7; paraphrased). Adam and Eve sinned. They also turned over their authority in the earth to Satan, the enemy of mankind, the enemy of God.

All people born after Adam and Eve inherit their sin and are born with a sin nature and a sin debt. All people, through no fault of their own, also inherit the punishment—physical and spiritual death. According to Isaiah, "Your iniquities have separated between you and your God, and your sins have hid his face from you, that he will not hear" (Isaiah 59:2). But God! What powerful words. But God, before the foundation of the earth, knew what would happen. God would not and did not leave humanity in sin and without hope. Because of His love for His creation, He planned that Christ would come to earth, live as a man, and die on a cruel cross to redeem people from their sin nature and sin debt. Jesus Christ was to pay the ultimate price, and He did. He became the perfect sacrifice, the lamb without blemish, required under Mosaic law. He paid your sin debt. He paid mine. As Paul points out, "For as in Adam all die, even so *in Christ* shall all be made alive (1 Corinthians 15:22, emphasis added).

The sacrifice of Jesus made it possible for everyone who accepts Him as Lord and Savior to be a "new creature," one whose old nature has been completely eradicated so that his life has "become new" (2 Corinthians 5:17). When this happens, those who have received

Christ's free gift of salvation can say with Paul, "*In him* we live and move and have our being" (Acts 17:28; emphasis added).

For most people in my generation and later who had Dos and Don'ts to govern their lives, their lists didn't work then; they don't work today. The practice simply gave people a checklist. As for me, I see now that I smugly checked off the Dos and Don'ts and felt very self-righteous about "keeping the laws." I compared myself with other people and declared that I was at least as good as most of them and better than some. I happily failed to see that my righteousness, in the eyes of God, is like "filthy rags" (Isaiah 64:6).

In my youth, not only did the majority of the preached messages come from the Old Testament (the Law), but a certain kind of "law" existed for those individuals caught in wrongdoing. If they were willing and obedient when they were confronted with their wrong-doing, church leaders asked them to stand in front of the church to confess their sins or wrongdoings and ask the church to forgive them. I became one of those individuals.

It happened one weekend when I was allowed to go on a double date, a blind date for me, with one of my girlfriends. She didn't tell me what the plan was, so I had no idea what we were going to do. After she and the two guys picked me up, we began to talk about what we would do as we drove toward town. They mentioned going to the movies, one activity that three of them favored. I kept quiet.

Immediately I began to be uneasy. I had been allowed to go to the movies with my dad as a child. In fact, he often loaded us girls up in the car and took us to the nearby drive-in theater. What a treat! Where was Mom? She stayed home because her church taught that seeing movies was sinful. So, by the time I was a teenager, my sisters and I had accepted Christ as our Savior. Dad no longer loaded us up to go see a movie; he didn't want to contribute to our "backsliding."

Now, here I was with a choice to make. My mind told me I couldn't hang out with this guy I didn't know at the little soda shop in town and listen to the juke box for the length of time that a movie would last. I didn't want to tell the rest of the group I couldn't go. After all, my dad had taken us as kids, and Mom didn't object. Even though I didn't agree with the church rule, I didn't want to break it. I didn't feel I could defend it. I was afraid to break it. But my pride also acted up. I didn't want to be viewed as the prudish "Miss Goody Two Shoes." So,

I broke the rule. With my heart hammering in my chest, I went to the theater and sat through the movie.

To this day, I can remember the misery of that evening! All I remember about the movie is that a western of some sort was showing. I couldn't enjoy any of it. I sat there almost suffocating with fear—a battle raging in my mind. Worry that the Lord might decide to rapture His devout saints away while I was there consumed me. I firmly believed that if the Lord should return or if I died during that movie, I would undoubtedly be lost. I could go to hell according to the preaching I had heard all of my life up to that time.

Finally, mercifully, the movie ended. I had not died. The Lord had not raptured the church. As far as I knew, no one from the church had seen me going in or coming out. I breathed a small sigh of relief as we stopped at the popular soda shop with a jukebox. All of us ordered a Brown Cow, but my favorite mixture of root beer with chocolate ice cream floating in it did not ease my mind. For the first time in my life, it was a relief to have an early curfew. I didn't have much time to socialize and engage in small talk, but I surely didn't want to face my parents with a story that I had gone to the movies. I couldn't bear the thought of disappointing them. After all, I was supposed to be a Christian role model for my dad now. Luckily for me, they were in bed by the time I got home. I had a reprieve—at least until morning. Sunday morning.

Exhausted from my emotional battle and feelings of self-condemnation, I slept fitfully. By morning my misery had multiplied exponentially. Inevitably, Mom and my sisters would ask about my date. When Mom asked, I told her some of the truth. She had already seen that my date was not the tall, dark, and handsome young man of my dreams. No need to embellish that. He was not good at conversation; I was worse that night. So, I told her what I thought was safe: I mentioned sitting at the soda shop, sipping Brown Cows, feeding the jukebox, and driving around a bit. I conveniently left out the rest. At that time, I thought I was safe. I had not yet learned what it meant to equivocate. I didn't know that I was a liar by omission. But, I had two reasons to dread arriving at church: I felt compelled to confess to my pastor, but I hadn't yet told Mom.

Without saying another word to my mother, I made a beeline for my pastor, my grandmother, at church time. In her usual desire to be on time to church, Mom insisted that we had to arrive almost thirty minutes before the appointed time. So, I had plenty of time to talk with Grandma before Sunday school started. Trembling inside to think that I had disappointed her and my church, I drew her aside and confessed that I had been to see a movie the night before and that I felt bad about it.

I really can't remember much about her reaction to my confession except her desire to protect me and the church. All I remember about that morning is what I read as her disappointment in my failure and her concern that someone who attended the church might have seen me go in or come out of the theater. She insisted that my being there could hinder my testimony and my ability to continue a teaching ministry at the church. Gently but firmly, Pastor Grandma advised that I needed to stand in front of the church and confess what had happened and ask them to forgive me. I should do that at the very beginning so as not to disturb Sunday school and worship.

Wanting to die, I silently prayed that the floor of the church would open up and the earth would swallow me alive. God did not answer that prayer. Nevertheless, afraid of God's wrath and in anguish at my grandmother's disappointment in me, I did exactly what she required. I stood before those people and confessed what I had done. Barely able to talk because of the tears of fear and remorse, I asked them to forgive me. I didn't dare look at my mother, but from the corner of my eye I saw her wipe tears from her eyes.

That one act was one of the hardest things I have ever had to do in my life. It was good medicine, though. I learned that I could do those things I feared to do if necessary. I could put my misery behind me and "face the music" of my choices. I never saw another movie in a theater for the next fourteen or fifteen years, and then it was only to take my English classes to see *Hamlet* or another of Shakespeare's plays made into movies. It was not for my personal entertainment until I embarked on Bible studies to learn for myself what God's Word teaches with the help of the Holy Spirit to interpret what I read.

Why do I mention this incident and the Dos and Don'ts? Because they informed my life journey. They are part of the system that governed my spiritual life into my adulthood and still intrude without warning. I have spent the last half of my life, to paraphrase Linda Christensen ("Unlearning the Myths That Bind Us"), unlearning the laws that bound me.

Chapter 6

UNLEARNING

If the Son therefore shall make you free,
ye shall be free indeed.

–John 8:36

————◈————

M any times I've thought I had arrived, that my battle with "religion" was over. Then something else would rear its ugly head.
I can imagine that you may be involved in the same kind of battle, that
just when you think you have accomplished the unlearning, you find
your mind bombarded again with "religious" notions and rules. The
stretch from law to grace has been cumbersome for me and for others,
too, I suspect. I have experienced that legalism and tradition allow the
stretch for a short time, but all too often I've found that parts of that
belief system snapped me right back to the place I've been trying to
leave behind. It's almost like an addiction. I've not been able to let
down my guard. I've had to be consistent and fight the good fight of
faith against tradition and the legalism that faces so many others.

A relationship with Christ will set you free; religion will keep you
bound. If your background has been like mine and you want to leave
it behind, you must be persistent. You must allow the Holy Spirit to
work in your mind and heart while you devour the Word of God with
an insatiable appetite. Your mind, gripped by years of training in tradition, must be saturated with Scriptures accompanied by prayer and
worship to break the grip and accomplish the retraining.

The apostle Paul gives clear direction in Romans 12: 2 when he says,
"Be not conformed to this world: but be ye transformed by the renewing
of your mind." "Renewing your mind"? What does that mean? Why is

it important? The New Testament, particularly the writing of Paul and Peter, will help find the answers to those questions.

In this part of his letter, Paul is encouraging the converts at Rome (and those of us who are reading the same Scripture today) to have the mind of Christ in various relationships. This "mindedness" causes those who love God to be clothed with humility, to obey Him, and to choose to do His will in all things—as Jesus did. Until we put on the mind of Christ, our first thought is of ourselves, our wishes, our plans. Me. Me. Me. With the mind of Christ, our focus changes, and we find real JOY, the real joy that comes from putting *J*esus first, *O*thers second, *Y*ourself last. It's not easy to do, but it's so worth it.

Another step to accomplishing a renewed mind is to search the Scriptures for and depend on the Holy Spirit to guide an understanding. Over the years, I've learned not to wait for scriptural understanding to be unearthed by a governing hierarchy and passed down to the obedient church members. I've discovered the importance of prayerfully studying the Word and depending on the Holy Spirit Himself for illumination.

The only part of an individual that changes at the new birth is the human spirit. According to Scripture, you and I are made up of three parts: spirit, soul, and body (1 Thessalonians 5:23). As a spirit being, we live in a body, and we possess a soul—our mind, our will, and our emotions. It's our spirit that becomes the new creation—something that never existed before Christ's redemptive work in us. Through our faith in His saving grace, we become "one spirit with Him" (1 Corinthians 6:17).

Can you grasp the concept of being one spirit with God Almighty? It seems, at first consideration, too good to be true. Contemplating this truth can bring you to your knees again and again. But that specific work of the Holy Spirit is only the beginning for you who accept Christ as Savior and Lord. So Paul gives instructions to "present your bodies a living sacrifice, holy, acceptable unto God" (Romans 12:1). A sacrifice has no choice in how its parts are to be used. You offer your hands to be used as He sees fit; you offer your feet to go where He says go. You learn the importance of guarding your eyes and ears so that whatever enters those gates to the mind help to build a relationship with God and do not clog it with noise and debris that get in the way of your devotion to and obedience to the Lord.

Paul also addresses temptations and recognizes the dangers ahead for believers. He warns the born-again Christians at Rome not to allow this world to mold them to its standards. Rather than remaining as they were prior to conversion, they should be "transformed [undergo a complete change] by the renewing of [their] mind" (Romans 12:2). Like the caterpillar that undergoes a metamorphosis and becomes a beautiful butterfly with the freedom of the skies, so will the Christian who has experienced the metamorphosis Paul talks about experience freedom from those things that had bound him to his "stinkin' thinkin.'"

The soul of the new believer does not automatically become new. Neither does the body. If you're born again while you're fat and feisty, you'll remain that way—at least until you adopt practices and beliefs that allow you to change your attitude and your size. If you tend to be strong-willed and argumentative, that won't change just because you've accepted Christ as your Savior. If you're caught up in bitterness and self-pity or your mindset says, "I'm from Missouri, so you have to show me," then your mind needs a makeover. Paul's word to the church in Rome addresses the mind; it leaves readers with a command, not a request, to retrain or renew our minds. This renewing is something that apparently requires your action and mine. However, how to achieve the desired results presents a dilemma and a challenge to many Christians.

Both Paul and Peter speak to the quandary of a renewed mind. Paul addresses the necessity when he encourages the church at Ephesus to "be renewed in the spirit of your mind" (Ephesians 4:23) and the church at Philippi to "let this mind be in you, which was also in Christ Jesus" (Philippians 2:5). Paul recognizes that the mind has its own "spirit," its viewpoint or mindset. According to his words, that mind needs to be renewed—made new all over again. Made new? Again? In this context, Paul stresses the necessity of mentally aligning with God's truth. This alignment begins at conversion, and believers must pursue it intentionally throughout their lives.

Paul clearly believed that individuals have a part in renewing their minds. He encourages his protégé Timothy to *study* to show himself approved of God while he "rightly divides" the word of truth (2 Timothy 2:15). To "rightly divide" the Scripture is to read it in context, to know what belongs under the law and what belongs under grace, what is directed to one group of people and what is directed to all believers whether Jew or Gentile. It is a disservice to the Word of God to read a verse out of context and then try to make a doctrine out of it.

It's also a mistake to read any portion of the Bible out of context and then to declare that the Word contradicts itself. It does not.

Perhaps Peter gives the more practical admonition, more practical to his audience at least: "Wherefore gird up the loins of your mind, be sober, and hope to the end for the grace that is to be brought unto you at the revelation of Jesus Christ" (1 Peter 1:13). This statement may have had more meaning to those who lived in his era and general location.

In his choice of words, Peter uses words similar to those of Paul, who tells us how to get ready for spiritual battle: "Stand therefore, having your loins girt about with truth, and having on the breastplate of righteousness" (Ephesians 6:14). Using the imagery of a Greco-Roman soldier dressing in battle gear, Paul warns Christian believers to put on the full armor of God so they can be fully protected in their battles. Peter, likewise, implies preparation for battle or other effort in his choice of language as he also paints a mental picture of the movements of a male citizen or a soldier getting ready to move into action.

In the culture of Peter and Paul, men wore long flowing robes that tended to get in their way when they were not simply lounging and enjoying fellowship while waiting for a meal to be prepared or to eat that meal. When they went into action, soldiers and other male citizens had to belt those robes or tuck them into a girdle around their waists, thereby causing their long robes to be drawn up out of their way. When they were thus "girded," they were ready for action.

A vital area Peter warns about protecting and keeping whole is mental capacity. He sees the importance of not allowing our minds to become vulnerable to traditions and other wrong influences of the past and the present. When he warns, "Be sober," he is not simply telling Christians not to be intoxicated on alcoholic beverages. He reminds us not to allow our imaginations to go wild, not to allow fears or unholy passions to hold us hostage. Was he also warning us not to accept others' thoughts and ideologies as our own without weighing them against the Word of God? I believe he was.

Even Jesus uses similar imagery as He teaches His followers to be ready and watchful for his return. He says, "Let your loins be girded about, and your lights burning" (Luke 12:35). The implication of His words is the same: Don't let your preparation for what's ahead get too casual and relaxed. Be constantly ready to fight the good fight of faith and to welcome His return. The truth of God's Word is the perfect armor for the battle that rages so much of the time. I agree with

Joyce Meyers (*Battlefield of the Mind*): the mind is where most of our battles occur. That's where Eve's downfall begins. All Satan has to do is to plant a thought; she's hooked. Centuries later, the mind of Jesus obviously needs protection when the devil tempts Him in the wilderness. In every case, Jesus responds with, "It is written" followed by Scripture. Those who constantly fill and refill their minds with God's Word can also answer with what they know to be in Scripture. They, too, can say, "It is written."

When we first come to Christ, our minds are filled and influenced with all the ideas and opinions we have ever heard or read: experiential learning, parental training, educational training, entertainment, and the like. These influences result in a lens—a mindset, sometimes called a frame of reference—that is geared toward our "flesh," the person we were before we got saved, the person with appetites for the things of the natural world and little interest in things of the spiritual world. That natural mindset is not wiped away when we come to faith in Christ. It continues and wars with the new creation that we become when we get saved until *we* do something about it. Just as the soldier or police officer or fire fighter is responsible for putting on the necessary protective gear, so are we followers of Christ responsible for making provision for the protection of our minds by maintaining an alertness and awareness of our own thought life and thoughts others are feeding us.

Simply put and based on my reading of Scripture, renewing your mind involves finding out who God is, whose you are, and who you are in Christ. In the process, you are taking on the mind of Christ. In his letter to the church at Philippi, Paul says, "Let this mind be in you, which was also in Christ Jesus" (Philippians 2:5). His words express a command, not a wish.

Letting the mind of Christ "be" in us is something we can't leave completely up to Holy Spirit. We have something to do, an action or a series of actions. First of all, we set ourselves to find out what the mind of Christ is like. We have the privilege of becoming acquainted with His mind. How does that happen? Very much the same way we come to know a spouse or a child or friends. When we spend time with them, listen to their thoughts and their dreams, and pay attention to what they say and how they say it, we become acquainted with their minds. By the same token, when we spend time reading the written Word and recognizing that the Word was made flesh and lived among men (John 1:14), we become familiar with the mind of Christ. As we read with purpose and spend time talking with and listening to the Savior, His mind becomes clearer to us.

Paul make it clear: it's up to you and me to renew our minds. That renewal is not optional. The Bible expresses how we accomplish the renewal in a number of ways. First, we look into and see "the light of the glorious gospel of Christ" (2 Corinthians 4:4); then, we hunger and thirst for righteousness with an unquenchable appetite (Matthew 5:6). That hunger and thirst will cause us to search the Scriptures and meditate on them until they become a part of us. As we see Christ in the Scriptures and learn more of Him, we begin to be transformed into His likeness. We bring down strongholds of human reasoning and false arguments and subject them to Christ (2 Corinthians 10:5).

As your mind is renewed, you learn to think as He thinks. Your hunger, thirst, and searching will stretch and stretch and stretch you. It is a process that continues for life as you counteract the world's thoughts and opinions as well as those that past traditions and practices continually try to interject. It will be the same for everyone who desires to be more like Jesus and to think like Him. The reward is a peace that comes with obedience, a sense of well-being, a sense of being in tune with your Maker.

Jesus is not a legalist. Although He came to earth and ministered under the Law, a list of rules and regulations that God gave and that Scripture describes as "holy, and just, and good" (Romans 7:12), God had a different plan from the foundation of the earth. He implements that different plan with the birth, life, death, and resurrection of Jesus Christ. By His unselfish death, Jesus pays the sin debt we inherited from Adam and redeems "us from the curse of the law" (Galatians 3:13). Paul declares that "we are delivered from the law . . . that we should serve in newness of spirit and not in the oldness of the letter [of the law]" (Romans 7:6), that we are no longer "under the law, but under grace" (Romans 6:14).

Following a list of Dos and Don'ts (the law of Moses) didn't renew the minds of the early church. It didn't prepare them to win the battles of the mind. Rules and regulations won't prepare us either. A vibrant relationship with Christ will. Knowing and understanding the Word of God will. The choice is ours. We choose to learn more of Him and His ways and let that knowledge transform us, or we choose to continue to walk in the mindset controlled by our flesh.

Did I keep all the "laws"? Not exactly. Did I spend most of my life as "Miss Goody Two Shoes"? You can be sure I did. I was afraid not to. I wanted to steer as clear of hell as possible—at least as far away as my understanding would carry me. I still do, but I'm now aware that God, not me, is the source of righteousness and holiness. Scripture tells me that my own righteousness and yours are as "filthy rags" (Isaiah 64:6).

At the risk of becoming redundant, I'd like to emphasize the "why" again. Why is it important to renew your mind? Well, to recap, Scripture tells us to do so. I remind you that Paul encourages believers: "Don't copy the behavior and customs of this world, but let God transform you into a new person by changing the way you think. Then you will learn to know God's will for you, which is good and pleasing and perfect" (Romans 12:2 NLT).

Copying the behavior and customs of this world is second nature to the unrepentant person who has not been renewed or transformed. According to Scripture all of us inherited Adam's sin nature. We need to become new, to be born again—as Jesus told a man called Nicodemus (John 3:1–5). True followers of Christ experience a phenomenal change: when they are born again, they are brought from death to life. That change takes place in the spirit. The person who comes to Christ in repentance and faith becomes a new person, changed into someone who never existed before (2 Corinthians 5:17). However, it is the spirit man that changes. The soul and body don't get the renewal at the same time or rate.

Before we come to Christ, wrong thinking grips us. To become the complete new person that Paul speaks of requires changing the way we think. We change the way we think by learning how God thinks. We learn how God thinks by hungering and thirsting for His righteousness and satisfying that hunger and thirst by feeding on His Word and His presence. It is only then possible to discover the "good, and acceptable, and perfect, will of God" (Romans 12:2). That's a good reason to renew the mind. Couple that reason with the knowledge that God's Word commands us to do so, and our great desire is to please Him. We also have to understand that the renewal is not an event; it is a process. The success of the process depends largely on our taking four steps:

(1) **Guarding the gates of the mind**. Wandering eyes and itching ears open to pornography and other ungodly practices and ideas promoted in movies, books, TV shows, the internet—all of these

things drag down the Christian and keep him or her from experiencing God's best and fulfilling His purpose. These things are soul pollution. They cause the "rivers of living water" that flow from deep within us (John 7:38) from the time we're born again to become clogged with this world's debris.

(2) **Bridling the tongue** so that it is not loose at both ends. Use of profane and vulgar language choices, lying, gossiping, promoting division—all of these things help to keep the mind in its original state and hinder a Christian's witness. The fruit of the spirit cannot flourish when it's crowded out by the uncontrolled desires of the flesh.

(3) **Exercising self-control and focusing on the right things**, things that are true, honest, just, pure, lovely, of good report, virtuous, and praiseworthy (Philippians 4:8) will keep followers of Christ from fulfilling lustful and greedy desires.

(4) **Knowing and obeying the Word of God.** As the prophet Samuel tells King Saul, "To obey is better than sacrifice" (1 Samuel 15:22). Samuel also warns that rebellion and disobedience are as sinful as witchcraft (1 Samuel 15:23). We cannot obey what we don't know. At the same time God does not condone ignorance of His word (Acts 17:30). When we learn and obey God's Word, we avoid caving in to a desire to "look good" to other people or to do it our way. Our obedience gains for us freedom from guilt and condemnation. More importantly, our obedience to the Word of God and the still small voice of Holy Spirit gains for us God's promised blessing (Deuteronomy 28).

Chapter 7

IMPUTING RIGHTEOUSNESS

Blessed is the man to whom
the Lord will not impute sin.
–Romans 4:8

———◆———

From the time I began to toddle around the house exploring my surroundings, I was taught to count. Fingers and toes. Red, blue, green, and yellow blocks. Pieces of pie. Socks in the drawer. The parts of the clover in our front yard. About the time of the onset of puberty, I moved on to count what friends had that I didn't as well as the wrongs I perceived had been inflicted on me. Soon I nursed feelings of inadequacy and grudges for those wrongs. My record of the number of wrongs always outweighed the acts of kindness—or so it seemed.

To extend the record-keeping to my budding spiritual life proved almost too easy. Very few sermons focused on the love of God and His life within us. Memorable sermons about hell's fire and brimstone, frequent focus on the failure of Israel to measure up to God's expectations over the centuries, and comparisons of Israel, God's chosen people, with God's modern-day church abounded. These kinds of messages from the pulpits of my childhood convinced me that God was an even more exacting taskmaster than my own very strict dad. I knew when I missed the mark. I kept record. Just as I confessed my movie-going to the church and asked them to forgive me, I tried to eradicate that record with good deeds. But I never could be sure just how many good deeds were required to make up for one bad one.

One of my problems was, in retrospect, how I saw God. I may have a faulty memory about a good many things, but I know one thing. I grew up in church, and, somewhere along the way, I developed a unique picture of God. Instead of seeing God as a loving Father, my mind's eye almost always conjured a picture of a faceless figure in a long, hooded garment with a scythe in his skeletal hand. This hooded figure's name? The Grim Reaper. Those whose authority I acknowledged, those whom I loved and respected, taught me that God keeps a record of all my wrongdoings. I had seen that image representing death somewhere on a relative's wall. That image appealed to my imagination. At any rate, that's how I began to see God. Perhaps the image solidified as I heard teaching on the parable Jesus told about wheat and tares. His story goes like this:

> The kingdom of heaven is likened unto a man which sowed good seed in his field: But while men slept, his enemy came and sowed tares among the wheat, and went his way. But when the blade was sprung up, and brought forth fruit, then appeared the tares also. So the servants of the householder came and said unto him, Sir, didst not thou sow good seed in thy field? from whence then hath it tares? He said unto them, An enemy hath done this. The servants said unto him, Wilt thou then that we go and gather them up? But he said, Nay; lest while ye gather up the tares, ye root up also the wheat with them. Let both grow together until the harvest: and in the time of harvest I will say to the reapers, Gather ye together first the tares, and bind them in bundles to burn them: but gather the wheat into my barn." (Matthew 13:24–30)

As ministers preached this parable from time to time, I came to see God as the man who planted a field of wheat. His enemy, Satan, planted weeds (tares) that grew up with the wheat. I could not help seeing myself as one of the weeds as I listened to sermon after sermon on hell's fire and damnation and God's judgment. The books the Lord opened at the Great White Throne judgment (Revelation 20:12–13) intrigued me and, at the same time, haunted me. Eventually, I learned that one of the books was the Book of Life with the names of the "saved" recorded in it; the other books contained the things by which people were to be judged. I thought they contained the listings of all the things I had ever done wrong in my life. Surely my life was so full of sins that I would not be gathered to keep. Instead, I was sure that I was a weed. The thought scared the daylights out of me. I tried harder to keep the rules and wept when I missed the mark. My mind and my training told me I would just have to work harder and do better.

When this Grim Reaper wasn't busy writing my sins in His book, He was walking around with a scythe in hand just looking for an opportunity to cut me and other sinners like me down and burn us on his scrap heap of unproductive weeds. No matter how much I prayed, no matter how many chapters I read in the Bible daily, in my eyes, I fell short. In my mind, I could hear God say to me at the Great Judgment, "Depart from me. I never knew you." Fear dominated my life. I was sure that I could never measure up.

A. W. Tozer said, "What comes into our minds when we think about God is the most important thing about us." So it seems that the most important thing about me then and for many years to come was that I was gripped by fear. The fear of God was the worst, but other fears also dominated my life: fear of failure, fear that I would not be a good wife and mother, fear of dying, fear that I would not make it to heaven. That perfect love that casts out all fear (1 John 4:18) escaped me. At that time in my life and for many years afterward, I could not shake the picture of God as the Grim Reaper.

Those same well-meaning and loving people who accepted the responsibility for keeping watch over my soul somehow had failed to emphasize or I had failed to grasp that God's Word teaches that He casts our sins into "the depths of the sea" (Micah 7:19), that He remembers those sins no more. I was well into the second half of my promised years before I began to feel secure in Christ, before I could accept that He alone—without my help—had made possible my salvation. Nothing I could do or needed to do beyond accepting His sacrifice and believing in Him could assure my eternal security. And wonder of wonders! If there was nothing I could do to earn my salvation, was it possible there was nothing I could do to lose it?

With that question, I faced another faith dilemma. Didn't I have to confess my sin, ask forgiveness, and repent every time I missed the mark? Didn't I have to get saved all over again? My training said I did. My training also provided for an unspoken hierarchy of sins.

The hierarchy provided for "little sins" like white lies and foul language and participating in the forbidden recreation. It recognized "big sins" like murder, pedophilia, adultery, fornication, perversions, molestations, and many others. In spite of being reared to believe in the ability of the little sins to send a believer to hell, my observation of adults that I admired and trusted revealed their tendency to get caught up in some of those "little sins." Many of them left out some of the whole truth if that served their purposes; they attended church when it pleased them; they let offense drive them from God and their church. Little sins versus big sins. Then there were sins I discovered in the Bible that were never mentioned in the pulpits of my youth—sins like gluttony, gossip, and "raising a ruckus," also known as stirring up strife among family members or members of the church. Why did no one preach against these sins?

Though I had read the Scriptures many times, I was already into middle age when I "saw the light," at least part of it. My head began to understand that when you come to Christ in faith, that

> if thou shalt confess with thy mouth the Lord Jesus, and shalt believe in thine heart that God hath raised him from the dead, thou shalt be saved. For with the heart man believeth unto righteousness; and with the mouth confession is made unto salvation. (Romans 10:9- 10)

The New Living Translation says it this way:

> when you openly declare that Jesus is Lord and believe in your heart that God raised him from the dead, you will be saved. For it is by believing in your heart that you are made right with God, and it is by openly declaring your faith that you are saved. (Romans 10:9–10)

The light bulb came on, first in my mind and then in my heart. Based on my faith in Him and my confession of faith, He delivers me *from* something *to* something else.

Let's take a rabbit trail for a minute. While I am not a Greek scholar by any means, I have learned to use reference material that helps me gain understanding in some exciting Bible "finds." For instance, that word *saved* in Romans 10:10 has its history in the Greek word *sozo,* which, according to Strong's Concordance, means "to save, deliver, protect, heal, preserve, do well, and be made whole." So, based on His promise and an understanding of the Greek word, I deliberately assure you that Christ has delivered us:

> *from* the bondage of our sins *to* new life in Christ and God's promises.

Through Him and because of Him we now can count on him for deliverance:

> *from* the bondage of addictions and sins *to* freedom;

> *from* fear and anxiety *to* peace and joy in the Holy Spirit;

> *from* sickness, disease and deformities *to* healing, wellness, wholeness, and completeness;

> *from* a high maintenance, high-strung personality *to* meekness and gentleness of spirit;

> *from* lack or poverty *to* material provision for ourselves and enough to help someone else;

> *from* what the enemy means for evil *to* protection and preservation.

It's a cliché in Christian circles today to call the Creator of the universe awesome. He does, surely, carry us beyond the colloquial meaning of "impressive" so many use today. He inspires awe and an overwhelming feeling of reverence. Sometimes, because we don't know any better, we even say what He does is incredible. Do we really want to say God is all that? I do, indeed, find Him and His works astonishing, extraordinary, and mind-boggling. However, "incredible" also means unbelievable, absurd, implausible, and inconceivable. None of those words describe Him. He is the One we can count on when we can't count on anyone else in the world. He is faithful beyond our wildest dreams. We can count on His compassions which never fail

(Lamentations 3:22–23). To be able to receive His *sozo* by faith seems almost too good to be true. But it is true!

The Bible says that if we accept Christ's sacrifice by faith we are made the righteousness of God in Christ (Romans 3:22; 2 Corinthians 5:21). We are made right the minute we place our faith in Jesus Christ; not only are we made in His image, but we also possess God's moral state of perfection. Our sins are no longer imputed to or counted against us. Think about that. Our sins—past, present, and future—no longer count against us? Past, present, *and future?* My heart has received this good news with gladness. My mind still has trouble taking it in sometimes. It's almost too much of a stretch.

The seeds of legalism are not easily uprooted. They are too much like the banana trees that we found at the last house we bought. They were overrunning everything else in our plant beds. We didn't like them, so we cut them down and tore them up by the roots. What roots we couldn't pull up we dug up. Through the late summer and fall and into winter we fought them. It was a long and arduous process, but we finally annihilated all the vestiges of banana trees. Or so we thought.

We never saw any more of them the rest of that summer and fall, but it was September by the time we thought they had been demolished. In December, we couldn't find any. The next spring brought another story. In the back of the house where they had been most prolific, we found a shoot of a banana tree growing up into and through the siding of the house. It had made a hole in the siding. Very much like sin in an unguarded life or the seeds of legalism grown to maturity, the roots of that that small forest were still underground. Again we had to pull and dig and spray with weed killer. It took nearly a year of fighting to get rid of all the roots and shoots.

Just as it was difficult to remove the unwanted plants, it is difficult to rid yourself of the roots and shoots of "religion." How can it be? He does not count my sins! He does not count your sins once you have accepted Him as Lord and Savior. Truth or fiction? Well, for the legalist who trusts in tradition and religion, it is fiction; for the believer in grace, it is truth. *Truth!* It is biblical. It is the promise of God. Paul assured the church at Corinth, "All the promises of God in him are yea [yes], and in him Amen [so be it]" (2 Corinthians 1:20). In the same letter he declared, "If any man be in Christ, he is a new creature: old things are passed away . . . all things are become new . . . God was in Christ, reconciling the world unto himself, not imputing their trespasses unto them" (2 Corinthians 5:17, 19).

For the person committed to keeping Dos and Don'ts, these verses are a real stretch. For those who have been introduced to grace, the Bible, once again, beckons them to move out of their traditions and flawed mindsets and to see with a new set of lenses. For those willing to be led of the Holy Spirit, His Word also holds a promise of deliverance. *Yes* means yes! *Yea* (KJV) means yes! Not maybe. Not perhaps. Not "psych" (meaning "fooled you." And I'm showing my age again).

However, these and other promises of God to us are conditional. While He has made precious promises regarding our deliverance, those promises require our faith in what He promised and our acceptance of the "so be it" imbedded in the word *Amen*. We read His Word, discover the promises and provisions that He has made through Jesus Christ and appropriate them. Receive them. Take them. Trust Him, especially the promise that He no longer counts our sins against us. And we rest in that promise. Stretching? For many of us, certainly.

While we have these precious promises, and I believe in the possibility of eternal security, I also believe the Bible supports that anyone can throw in the towel and renounce the Lord. Some people accept Christ as Lord and Savior, and somewhere along their life's way they become cold and unresponsive in their walk with Him. A loss, a disappointment, a dream unfulfilled—any number of things can derail the believers who allow their passion for Christ to cool. Those Christians then sometimes fall prey to the temptation to override the still small voice of the Holy Spirit who is trying to guide them. They refuse the Lord's directions until their hearts become hardened and unresponsive to His Word (Hebrews 3:7–13). Those who have experienced salvation by grace through faith can surely reroute themselves.

And in case you think that I believe that God's grace gives us a license to live any way we want to live, I hasten to assure you that I do not. In Matthew 5:48 Jesus tells his disciples, *"Be ye* therefore *perfect*, even as your Father which is in heaven is perfect" (emphasis added).

Let's understand that His command here has little to do with the common understanding of *perfect* as we use it today. Most of the time, we use the word loosely to mean good looking (of a man or woman), satisfying our taste (of furnishings or layout for living), just the right temperature and strength (of a cup of tea or coffee), or a host of other ways. If we use the common English meaning in describing something, we mean the thing described is without flaw, not needing correction. In the context of Christ's command, this definition has the ability to throw sincere Christians into despair. How can I possibly live up to the description of "flawless" as a Christian? Strong's concordance, however gives hope in its definition of *perfect* as complete in all its parts; full grown, of full age; specially of the completeness of Christian character.

In the context of the Sermon on the Mount, the implication of our Lord's command is that we strive to attain full maturity and become living epistles that convey the attributes of a God of love; because of His love for us, we strive to love others as He loves us. In that sense, we allow Him to bring us to perfection or full maturity, not in an abstract sense, but in love for others, to love others in an unselfish and forgiving way. In other words, "be perfect in [your] love for one another" ("Be Ye Therefore Perfect." *The Biblical World*. Vol. 22, No. 4, Oct. 1903, pp. 243–247).

Chapter 8

FINDING THE TRUTH

And ye shall know the truth, and the truth shall make you free.
–John 8:32

—————◆—————

"Judith Lynn, look under the bed and see if Poppy's slippers are under there." Grandma Spencer's deep voice moved me to the side of the old iron bed that was neither a twin nor a full-sized bed. It was somewhere in between and sat higher off the floor than beds today.

Reluctantly I got on my knees and peered into the darkness under that bed. Near the wall, the full width of the bed from where I knelt, I spied the outline of Poppy's slippers resting among the dust bunnies. But it was so dark back there. Had the black beast whom Grandma named Twiffie and who, according to her, usually lived in the soot receptacle of the kitchen stove, escaped? Was he there hiding in the dark? With a shiver of fear that Twiffie, along with his comrade spiders and other creepy creatures of the darkness, might be lurking behind the slippers and shame for what I was about to say, I muttered in a small voice, "I don't see them, Grandma."

"Are you sure? Look again."

Fearing the creatures under the bed more than Grandma, I whined, "I can't see them."

"Judith Lynn," her stern voice admonished as she knelt beside me, "if I see those slippers under that bed, I'm giving you a spanking." Why did she threaten? Did she already know that the slippers were under the bed?

Once again, Grandma did not make idle threats. After retrieving them from the depths of darkness, Grandma used one of Poppy's slippers to tan my backside right then and there. With firm resolve, Grandma punctuated the importance of telling the truth—without abusing me. It was a memorable event. I learned something important from her that day. Grandma believed in speaking the truth; she tried to teach me to tell the whole truth and nothing but the truth, so help me God.

Over the years, I've fallen to the temptation to whitewash the truth for my own benefit or to equivocate as it seemed advantageous. Almost immediately, the Holy Spirit has prompted me to tell the unvarnished truth or to button the lips. In a day when so many public figures get caught up in lies and deceit, it is easy to fall into the same pit. After all, we are tempted to reason, "everyone does it." We employ the old excuse to ourselves if not to our audience. When politicians or other public figures have their lies made public, they and the general public seem to shrug it off. They cloak themselves with nonchalance. Since they are so unmoved by getting caught, does the public also react with apathy? It does seem so. However, the God of heaven has standards and encourages believers to line up with those standards—with His help!

Just prior to his crucifixion, Christ warns Peter that he will deny His Savior. A fervent Peter declares that will never happen. He obviously doesn't know himself very well, for after the soldiers take Christ captive and parade Him before Pilate and the Sanhedrin, Peter denies that he ever knew Christ—not once, not twice, but three times. One of those denials is accompanied by cursing for punctuation and emphasis. Just as soon as the rooster crows the third time, he remembers that his Lord predicted that he, the rock, would falter. With bitter anguish, Peter weeps and leaves the scene of the pre-crucifixion activities.

A very encouraging aspect of this story, another evidence that grace has been delivered to this world, is that Christ does not accuse Peter or give him a tongue lashing. He does not say, "I told you so." He does not rail at him or give him the silent treatment. Instead, grace and love in the person of Jesus Christ look on him with compassion. He does the same for us when we fail to live up to His standards. From time to time, I am tempted to enhance a story, to exaggerate for effect. Too often I have fallen to the temptation. Then I feel a nudge from the gentle Spirit to embrace truth, for Scripture says that Satan is a liar and the father of lies (John 8:44). God's Word asks, "What communion hath light with darkness?" (2 Corinthians 6:14). His Word then clarifies: "God is light; in Him is no darkness at all" (1 John 1:5). That Scripture, by inference, equates Satan with darkness.

The Bible also says, "Ye shall know the truth, and the truth shall make you free" (John 8:32); it declares that Jesus is "the way, *the truth*, and the life (John 14:6, emphasis added). Even joking about my age, saying that I'm going to be Jack Benny's age for the next forty years— just that bit of levity now feels inappropriate for the person that I know I am, one spirit with the truth. The truth and light come to live in you and me when we accept Jesus as Lord and Savior. Satan lies. His lot is lies and darkness. My lot and yours is truth and light.

The choice is ours. Choose light instead of darkness. Stretch to freedom.

Chapter 9

LEARNING TO PRAY

And all things, whatsoever ye shall ask
in prayer, believing, ye shall receive.
–Matthew 21:22

———◦◦———

F rom the time my memories start, Grandma Spencer preached the
gospel. In a day when hardly any mainstream denominational
churches recognized women as ministers of the gospel, she accepted
the call and the challenge. It didn't seem to deter her any that she was
a lonely woman in a man's world. Fearlessly, she answered the call
to preach. Male ministers were in short supply in West Virginia, so
female evangelists often pastored churches that were too small to support male pastors with wives and families. My grandmother was one
of those women.

Spending the night or a few days with Grandma excited me. With
three children born in just two years and eleven months, Mom had her
hands full. Grandma often relieved Mom's burden and took me to her
house where I felt special. It was at her knee that I first learned Bible
verses. It was by her side that I learned to pray. My sisters and cousins
may object to my claim, but I've always believed I was her favorite.

Kneeling beside her during the day and at bedtime, I heard her fervent prayers. As she lifted her voice to the heavens and called out to
God, sometimes in tones of agony, she mentioned every relative and
all her church members. She prayed for the country, for her sons in the
U. S. Navy, for her congregation, and for inspiration and anointing to
preach the Word of God. I listened more than I prayed. Even at an early
age, I wanted to pray like her—just as long and as loud, but I never
seemed to find as much to say as she did.

71

My learning to pray started small with a child's prayer, one that Grandma and Mom taught and supported. It was a bedtime ritual from the time I learned to talk. Kneeling at the side of the bed, my sisters and I were taught to make our childish requests known:

> Now I lay me down to sleep.
> I pray the Lord my soul to keep.
> If I should die before I wake,
> I pray the Lord my soul to take.

As I think about that prayer now, I shudder a bit at teaching little ones just barely able to talk the line about dying! I regret now that I taught my own children the same prayer. I didn't even think about how it might sound to a child. I didn't give one thought to what it might do their minds to focus on death every night of their young lives. I had not yet learned that I could teach my children to know a loving God, a God of life, a God who defeated death. I wish I had known the alternate version:

> Now I lay me down to sleep.
> I pray the Lord my soul to keep.
> May angels watch me through the night
> And waken me at morning light.

Eventually, I learned how to put prayer into my own words. From the prayers of my mom and my grandma, I figured out how to pray for various relatives and their needs. I prayed that my dad would "get saved." During a family crisis, I prayed for my little sister Carol who somehow managed to get dry beans into her nose and her windpipe. One made it into her lungs where it swelled. She was not yet two years old, and death tried to claim her. God heard my prayer asking Him not to let her die. He heard Mom's fervent prayer. He heard our unsaved uncle's prayer as he drove Mom and the baby at breakneck speeds the six or seven miles on curvy country roads to the nearest hospital in a little more than six minutes. God paid attention to Dad's promise to live for Him if He only would save his baby. She lived. So I also learned the summer before my fifth birthday to thank God for answered prayer.

I remember another fervent prayer at a young age; I must have been about seven years old. My dad had fulfilled his desire to have a motorcycle. He loved riding with the younger men of the community, men who didn't have wives and children. He was the only one among the three or four of his group to wreck—not once but three times. Two of the three wrecks jeopardized his life. In one of them someone he knew backed out of his driveway just as Dad was coming up to the curve in which his house sat. Dad thought the man did it on purpose. Even though I heard him say why he felt that way, I don't remember the reason. I just know we children prayed fervently alongside Grandma while Mom and her dad, Poppy George, went to the hospital to sit with Dad and pray by his bedside that he would live. Thankfully, God was merciful again.

All three wrecks occurred in less than a year. The worst of the three happened on a stretch of new highway. The road was not yet well-traveled. It was so new that the asphalt was fresh and bright; not a single skid mark marred its dark beauty. On each side, something called "red dog," a substance left at the coal mine when slate dumps caught fire and burned, covered the shoulder. A recycled material, red dog did not cost the state much. It was a popular material for the shoulders of the highways in West Virginia, a land of many coal mines in those days.

How did the wreck happen? It seems that my dad and several of his friends were busy laying down skid marks on the new highway. They were also clowning, and Dad always had to be the best and most daring at everything he did. So he decided to stand on his motorcycle seat and ride it down a small grade. Everything went as planned until he hit a stone in his lane, and the unguided motorcycle went out of control. In a few short seconds, life changed again for him. He wound up at the beginning of a culvert on the side of the road with part of the motorcycle on top of him. A front wheel, still moving, ground his face into the red dog. He had other injuries. At this time, I can't remember what they were, but I cannot forget my horror when I learned that he had one eye lying on his cheek, and one side of his nose had been ripped from his face so that half of it flapped. That picture was so hideous to my mind's eye that I have not been able to forget it.

Again Mom rushed to the hospital and left my sisters and me with Grandma. The next thing I knew Grandma was calling us to prayer for our Dad. She told us he was badly injured, that he might die. As she prayed, I noted that she was asking God to spare his life, to save him, to change him. So I joined her in the prayer that my dad would live and come back to God. God answered our prayers; He spared Dad's life. I heard Dad recognize that God had kept him, but he continued to live what Grandma and Mom called an "ungodly" life.

I can't remember a time when I didn't pray. I can, however, remember with great clarity that night at the little country church when I felt a definite call to repentance from the Holy Spirit. Even as a nine-year-old, I knew that I needed to accept Jesus as my Lord and Savior. I was a child who had been in church all her life; I wanted to answer the call, but I didn't want to go forward to the altar. I desperately wanted to pray. I just didn't want people to see me going forward.

Today, even after my personal experience, I find it hard to imagine that children could experience such a spiritual tug of war when they feel a call to repentance. But it was true for me. No doubt about it. I had a battle raging inside me. I wanted to kneel at the altar, but something tried to hold me back. "I can't" quickly eclipsed "I will." As conviction seized me, tears washed down my cheeks, but my feet did not budge. The evangelist stopped his exhortations, and musicians began to sing:

Just as I am without one plea,
but that thy blood was shed for me
and that thou biddest me come to thee,
O Lamb of God, I come. I come.

The song ended. With these words ringing in my ears, I heard the preacher say, "If you'll take the first step, Christ will take the next steps with you." The preacher's words were true then; they are just as true today. I can remember taking just one step. I found that when I took the first step, He met me. Suddenly I was at the altar asking God to forgive my sins and make me His child. After bathing it with my tears and promising to take Him as my Lord and Savior, I rose from the altar feeling different, lighter somehow. The heavy burden I had carried and the raging battle inside me during the altar call were gone. I could barely wait to tell my parents what had just happened to me, but they were not at church.

Dad was a Christmas, Easter, funeral, and wedding church-goer at that time so he was at home that night. So was Mom. Barely ten or twelve weeks pregnant with my third sibling, Mom was at home nursing a "morning sickness" that had no respect for the time of day. Both of them were in bed when Grandma and Poppy dropped me at home after church. I could wait no longer to tell them that I got saved that night. Overflowing with my good news and yet feeling an uncommon shyness, I tiptoed right up to their doorless bedroom covered only with a curtain to share what had happened. Mom told me to come in. She cried and hugged me. Dad never had much to say about religious things. My memory declares that he simply said, "That's good, Sis."

My two younger siblings gave their hearts to Christ a short time after that. So the women in our family were getting safe from hell. For the next thirty years, my sisters (who eventually numbered four) and I would join Mom and Grandma in prayer that my dad, who professed Christ when he and Mom married, would "get saved again." At the time in my life, many devout ministers, including my grandmother, believed and preached that anyone who had once known the Lord and strayed away from him had to get saved all over again. That's all she knew. That's what I learned. I learned it well.

Our family and our church had met grace in person, but we didn't yet know how God's grace worked in the day-to-day affairs of people who had "backslidden." If we did something contrary to the expressed articles of faith, if we "missed the mark" according to Scripture, didn't that mean that we were "sinners" and no longer Christ followers? That's what I believed fervently. What's worse, I weighed myself in the balances and always found myself lacking. I never seemed to be able to feel secure in His love. So, I religiously involved myself in every activity and joyfully agreed to take on every job offered or needed at the local church in an attempt to satisfy a God who described Himself as "jealous" (Exodus 20:5). Maybe, just maybe, my good works could outweigh my faults, failures, and sins. That was my abiding hope and unexpressed prayer. Unfortunately, my ability to trust my heavenly Father and His love for me continued to be bombarded by doubt that I could ever measure up to His standards.

Many Christians that I know continue under the same understanding. While many thousands, or hundreds of thousands perhaps, have begun to understand biblical grace, I know too many fervent Christians who are still struggling to earn their way to heaven. Even though the New Testament Scriptures that clearly define and exemplify God's grace have been in the Bible for centuries, the understanding still escapes people, most of whom want to please God at all costs. Jesus said,

> "My sheep hear my voice, and I know them, and they follow me: And I give unto them *eternal* life; and *they shall never perish, neither shall any man pluck them out of my hand*. My Father, which gave them me, is greater than all; and no man is able to pluck them out of my Father's hand." (John 10:27–29, emphasis added)

Thoroughly trained and rooted in religion or "legalism," I have grasped the Lord's words with great difficulty. Well, truth be told, over the years, I'd think I had grasped them, but just when I thought the matter was settled, I'd question again. "What about the sins I've committed since giving my heart to Christ? What about those people who continue to do the ungodly things they did before they asked Jesus into their lives?" Some will declare, "They were never saved!"

I questioned my understanding over and over. Even though He promised that He will never leave or forsake us, can't I leave Him? Can't you or I park Him in the car while we frequent the bars and get falling-down drunk? Can't we leave Him on the couch in the living room while we commit adultery in the bedroom? Can't I turn my back on Him while I steal from my employer or lie to my spouse about why I lost my job?

Without a doubt, you and I can decide to turn a deaf ear to the gentle nudging of the Holy Spirit. I can choose to squander my inheritance on "riotous living" and rummage in the pig pens just as the Prodigal Son did. You remember that story, don't you? Some people prefer to call it The Story of the Elder Brother. Some call it The Story of the Lost Son. But let's focus on the one we learned to call the "prodigal" for a bit. His story is told in Luke 15:11–32.

As Jesus tells the story, a wealthy man has two sons. For the sake of our discussion, let's put the story into modern terms and start by describing the older one as conscientious, dependable, and staid. The younger is a different creature. Unwilling to wait for his inheritance, and in selfish rebellion, he pressures his dad to give him his share of the family fortune so he can shake the dust of lackluster living off his feet and head to the city lights. In effect, according to the culture of Jesus's day, he is saying, "I wish you'd die so I can have my inheritance." So it happens. The father doesn't die, but he does divide his wealth between the two boys and gives each son the portion he should have received at a later time in his life. Each deserves it—just not at this particular time in his life. One son remains at home.

With the bounty of his father's hard work in his possession, the younger son sets out to find life in the city. Anywhere but on the farm. Anywhere but under the scrutiny of his father and his dull older brother. Right outside the safety of loving family, he plunges into a lifestyle for which he is ill-equipped, just as almost anyone reared by a loving parent and taught the ways of the Lord is not equipped for such a lifestyle. Free of loving restraints, he enjoys the pleasures of sin for a season. Fair weather friends abound. Hangers-on multiply. As long as the money lasts, wine, women, and song answer to his call. Then one day, the finite amount of money in his inheritance vanishes. Gone! So also vanish his so-called friends.

Where are the abundant numbers of friends? Isn't it time for them to share what they have with him? Everything he had he has spent on them. Now he is chillingly destitute. No money for shelter. Nothing left for food and clothing. No friends to take him in and feed him. His days pass in hopeless desperation as famine sweeps the land, and he begins to starve. Finally, someone hires him to feed their pigs. (We called it "slop the hogs" when I was growing up.) Misery turns into despair. To stave off starvation, he becomes willing to forage in what he feeds the pigs. Disgusting. Sickening. Anything but kosher. His circumstances force him to another crossroads, another challenge.

With a sick heart, he eventually comes to his senses and realizes that the servants at his father's house have better living conditions and food than he has. In a sudden burst of sanity, he decides to go back to his father's home. He purposes to tell his father, "I have sinned against heaven and you, and I am no longer worthy of being called your son. Please take me on as a hired servant."

The Bible doesn't tell us his thoughts as he travels. I imagine a scenario that could have played as his weary, malnourished body takes one tentative step after another closer to his father's house:

"What will Father think? Will he forgive my rebellion? Will he allow me to return? Did I blow every chance I have of a roof over my head and real, honest-to-goodness food to eat?"

Step after weary step, he covers the dusty road to what was once his home. Dreadful thoughts continue to bombard him as he labors to put one foot in front of another.

"Is the family still where I left them? What about my older brother? Will I suffer at his hands when I return? Will he always remind me of my selfishness? my indiscretions? my wastefulness? my stupidity?"

As he continues homeward, his mind refuses to be at ease. Uncertainty swirls in his head and holds his thoughts prisoner.

"If Father will just allow me to be his servant, I'll never ask for another thing from him. But, will he? That's the question. Has he disowned me for life?"

Perhaps he peers into the distance and remembers his lifestyle before he went away. He had clean clothes, plenty of food, a lavish home, standing in the community—everything he needed. He was somebody then.

"Look at me. I'm so filthy that I may not even be allowed in the servants' quarters."

Pause. . . .

"I don't know what to do. I just know I can't go on like this. I've got to trust my father. I hope he still loves me. God, please help me to make it home."

Step after weary step, the remorseful and physically wasted young man makes his way through the fields, over the rocky and dusty roads, up one hill and down another. The distance seems interminable. Finding a rock, he rests his back against it as he contemplates what might await him: a cold, indifferent brother and an unforgiving father who has every right to lash out at him for his stupidity. Wanting to go anywhere but home, he considers his options.

"What options? I'm kidding myself. I have three choices: lie down and die from starvation, go back and beg the landowner to let me come back and feed the pigs, or go home and face the music. I'm not ready to die; I'm too young. Eating and living with the pigs was worse than horrible. I think I'll throw myself at my father's feet and beg his forgiveness. I'll just have to take whatever my brother dishes out. I must go home."

And so anxiety nearly consumes him as he puts one foot in front of the other. Eventually, the steps toward home bring him to a stunning sight. It stops him in his tracks. He has reached the edge of his father's fields, and someone is running in his direction.

"What? Who is that I see ahead? It looks like someone running. Oh, God, what's happening? What's he doing? Who is it? I must be hallucinating. Is it Father? Can he possibly be running toward me?"

Pause. . . .

"It is Father! It is! He is running! He has his arms outstretched towards me. Is that a smile on his face? It looks like he wants me. Now I can see better. He is smiling. Oh, God, thank you!"

Without further ado, the Prodigal Son continues wearily to his father who, casting aside his dignity, *runs* to envelop his lost son in his arms and his heart. With a shout of joy, he orders the servants to bring clean clothes and to prepare a feast in his honor. The son had been lost but now is found. The family and servants will celebrate his homecoming.

I can remember the first time the Spirit of God spoke to me in a still small voice about this story. Years after I first heard the story and had read it many times, I heard in my spirit, "The Prodigal Son never stopped being the son. Even in the pits of sin, He was the younger *son*." He has reminded me time and again that the wasteful young man was always a beloved son, even when he was out wasting his inheritance. When he came to his senses and turned from his rebellious ways, he found his father waiting to welcome him with open arms. He returned home to find rejoicing and celebration—except for the older brother. Gripped by outrage and jealousy, the older brother complained bitterly to his father that no one ever threw a party for him.

While it is possible to commiserate with the older son and empathize with his position, the treatment of the younger one has threatened to put me off balance. A few years ago, I was mulling this familiar story over again. From childhood, I had loved the story and found comfort in it, but it left me wondering why Jesus told that particular story. I thought it so beautifully illustrates a father's love and his willingness to take his repentant son back home, but my tradition put up a barricade to any further understanding. The spiritual significance escaped me.

But God came to my rescue, and the Holy Spirit spoke to me again causing a light bulb of understanding to switch on in my head. A comforting illumination. In my spirit I heard, "The Prodigal Son never ceased to be a son. Even when he was involved in riotous living, even when he was in the pig pens, he was still a son." Then I noted again that his father was watching daily for him to come home and ran to receive him when he did. Running was not dignified for an adult in his culture and station in life. But he ran. He welcomed the wasteful son back home. Then he made it possible for this dirty, unkempt, and irresponsible son to clean the filth from his body and change to the fresh clean clothing and grooming befitting his heir. He placed on this younger son's hand a new signet ring signifying restored authority in the family. He put new sandals on his feet; he ordered a celebration in honor of his return.

While remembering that parables tell a story that can stand alone but usually have a lesson embedded in them, I prayed for the wisdom of the Holy Spirit to give me an understanding of the spiritual lesson. As I meditated, it seemed that God's Spirit opened the eyes of my heart.

The father in this story represents our Heavenly Father who loves us dearly. Even when we deliberately fritter away our inheritance, He patiently watches for us to come to our senses. He meets us as we return to Him in repentance. We can trust Him to forgive us, to welcome us with loving arms, to change our "clothing," and to return the authority and power of sonship to us. That understanding comforted my spirit, but I still wondered what happens when I get my eyes off the prize? When I mess up? Again, I have to look to the wisdom of God's Word, which says that God Himself is the One who has established and anointed us; it is He who has, as Paul says, given us His protection from the contaminants of this world and has placed in us a partial payment of His promises. He calls that partial payment the earnest of the Spirit or His guarantee:

> in whom [Christ] ye also trusted, after that ye heard the word of truth, the gospel of your salvation: in whom also after that ye believed, ye were sealed with that holy Spirit of promise, Which is the earnest of our inheritance until the redemption of the purchased possession, unto the praise of his glory. (Ephesians 1:13–14)

The New Living Translation says it this way:

> And when you believed in Christ, he identified you as his own by giving you the Holy Spirit, whom he promised long ago. The Spirit is God's guarantee that he will give us the inheritance he promised and that he has purchased us to be his own people. He did this so we would praise and glorify him.

Then the truth of Scripture settles in around me like a warm blanket on a chilly night. Christ assures His disciples that no person on earth—not even they themselves—has the power to take them away from Him. No one, not even you or I, can remove us from His hands. He said so Himself. That's His blessed assurance to us in His words,

> "My sheep know my voice, and I know them. They follow me, and I give them eternal life, so that they will never be lost. No one can snatch them out of my hand. My Father gave them to me, and he is greater than all others. No one can snatch them from His hands, and I am one with the Father." (John 10:27–30 CEV)

That's also a part of the grace package Paul is talking about: "By grace you are saved through faith" (Ephesians 2:8). Scripture assures that no one can remove an individual believer, one of His sheep, from the Father's hands. That promise seals the gift of God that we have learned to call grace. Paul confirms the message in his first letter to the church at Corinth. He assures us that God has "sealed us, and given the earnest of the Spirit in our hearts" (2 Corinthians 1:22).

Those who have purchased a house or other property have no trouble understanding "earnest" in its modern context. When they look at the word in the context of money they have placed into the hands of a seller or the seller's agent as a sign of intent to buy a specific property, the biblical use of the word gains more meaning. That money offers the owner some assurance that the buyers are serious about their offer to purchase. In the same context, a seal helps to finalize the deal. The final evidence of ownership is a deed or a title on which is affixed the official seal of the official or government agency that has the authority to issue the document.

Using language that they would understand, Paul assures the church at Corinth and us today that Christ "has identified us as his own by placing the Holy Spirit in our hearts as the first installment that guarantees everything he has promised us" (2 Corinthians 1:22 NLT). That assurance is mine and yours when we come to Christ in faith, when we receive his promises by faith.

Two keys determine your success in this area:

1. You must come to Him in faith, for "without faith it is impossible to please him" (Hebrews 11:6).

That faith goes beyond mental assent. It surpasses simple belief that God is, that Jesus died to save you from your sins, that you can have eternal life. James tells us that even the devils "believe and tremble" (James 2:19). True faith requires your complete reliance on and trust in the Savior and His words. The story of a modern artist and entertainer illustrates that kind of faith.

Remember the story of the great tightrope walker from the Wallenda family? Although Nik Wallenda did, in fact, set many records as a tightrope walker, the story I remember may be as much legend as truth. In 2012, Wallenda set out to achieve another world record, this time performing a feat which had taken several years to plan; besides preparing the equipment, he also had to obtain permission from officials in the US and Canada.

Eventually, Wallenda's plans came to fruition. He had a wire placed across Niagara Falls. Then, at the chosen time and with a large crowd and scores of television cameras present, he carefully and with great difficulty inched across the falls. As the wind and the falls roared, mist threatened his vision. In spite of the possible pitfalls, he expertly balanced himself and took one small but confident step after another across the falls. Onlookers held their collective breath and let out audible sighs of relief each time he reached a milestone—down a hazardous slope, from American territory to Canadian jurisdiction, from the river to the falls and on to a crowd watching from below. Just watching must have been a harrowing experience, and the crowd of thousands waiting for him on the Canadian side erupted into wild cheers of acclamation when the journey ended and he was safe there in front of them. The rest of the story may or may not be true. I've been unable to verify it. However, it powerfully illustrates a biblical truth. Please allow me the benefit of a doubt as I tell it the way I heard it.

Grinning into the crowd on the Canadian side of the falls, Nik Wallenda is said to have asked his onlooking supporters if they thought he could do it again. They assured him of their belief in his expertise.

"Of course."

"No doubt."

"You can do it."

Different words of affirmation rang out in the crowd. Pausing just a moment, as if for effect, he then asked one of his assistants to bring him the wheelbarrow that was ready for his request. Balancing the wheelbarrow carefully on the tightrope, the consummate artist and entertainer then called out, "Who believes I can push this wheelbarrow across the falls?"

The crowd had just seen his success. They thought they believed he could do anything on the tightrope. They didn't pause long to answer. Soon other affirming voices began to be heard. Turning to a man standing just below his ladder, the celebrity asked, "Do you believe I can push this across the falls?"

"Of course," the man proclaimed with a smile and a loud voice. "I am sure you can do it."

"Then come and get in the wheelbarrow." The challenge rang out. A stunned crowd sucked in their collective breath once again—waiting for an answer. It was not forthcoming. Dropping his head, the man who had seemed so sure quickly tried to get lost in the crowd. After several more invitations, the matter was settled. Many claimed to believe he could push the wheelbarrow across the falls, but not one volunteered to get in the wheelbarrow.

The point of this story illustrates the second key to success.

2. True faith in God and in the finished work of Christ will cause us to get in His wheelbarrow and let Him navigate the falls of our lives.

One more important thing to remember here, though, is the need to be aware of the forces working in your life. You can have faith and start the journey with Jesus in complete faith and still be caught off guard in one area or another if you're not careful. Paul warns, "See to it that no one takes you captive by philosophy and empty deceit, according to human tradition, according to the elemental spirits of the world, and not according to Christ," (Colossians 2:8 ESV). James also offers godly advice about wisdom and its works. He says wisdom that does not come from God is "earthly, unspiritual, demonic" (James 3:15 NIV). He continues that jealousy and selfish ambition bring disorder and every vile practice, but he offers hope: "But the wisdom that is from above is first pure, then peaceable, gentle, and easy to be intreated, full of mercy and good fruits, without partiality, and without hypocrisy" (James 3:17).

Test the "wisdom" that comes to you against what the Bible says. Pray over it and ask God to enlighten the eyes of your understanding (Ephesians 1:18), to "open the eyes of your heart" so you can see what is true wisdom and what is not.

Wisdom and faith in God will inspire you, like Elisha, to leave family, animals, and lands behind and follow wherever He leads. You will experience no greater satisfaction and fulfillment in life than to find and follow the path God has laid out for you. You will be at peace and experience true contentment knowing that His plans trump your plans every day, that He is bringing to pass for you what He knows is best. Even when you consider that the path before you looks impossible to travel, your trust in Him will cause you to move forward.

Chapter 10

LEAVING THE NEST

Faith is believing in something when common sense tells you not to.
—from the movie "Miracle on Thirty-fourth Street"

———◦◦◦———

A t the tender age of seventeen, I set off to realize my dream. Even though my family's lifestyle did not support my position, in my mind's eye, I was as much "middle class" as anyone else. It didn't matter that we still lived in four rooms with a path; we had graduated to a basement blasted out of rock with dynamite. It had storage space and a working shower. It didn't matter that I shared with four sisters a small room big enough only for two sets of metal bunk beds and an army style cot for sleeping. It didn't matter that Dad just recently had piped water from the well into our kitchen. It didn't matter that we had postage stamp–sized public rooms not big enough to seat eight people comfortably in any one of them unless someone sat on the floor in the living room or we all sat at the kitchen table.

We managed. We had even found room in our small living room for a television set, one of the first in our community, when television was still pretty much in its infancy. We had radio. We had records and an old Victrola on which to play them. And, wonder of wonders, we even had an old pump organ. So, in my mind, we had enough for our needs and more. Food, shelter, clothing, and entertainment, all under one roof. And somehow, God would help me find a way to go to college. I never doubted it.

When I was in seventh grade, I had caught the attention of our elementary school principal, who also taught a few classes. He saw something in me that I had not yet recognized. Maybe it was my bossiness (Today I call it leadership ability.) or my desire to lead and be the best in every activity at each grade level. Several times he asked me to "teach" first and second graders when their teacher had to be out part of the day and he could find no substitute. It was a heady experience. I discovered that I loved being in charge of children besides my siblings. At least, those at school behaved better when I threatened to write a note to the principal. My siblings had not learned the art of obeying their big sister. They never did.

As a twelve-year-old, I also enjoyed teaching a class of small children during a vacation Bible school at my church. So, with no training and a load of desire I was introduced to my first ministry experience. I was hooked! I seemed to have found my calling. That first experience would lead, eventually, to surprising opportunities and appointments—all of them unpaid positions—unpaid, that is, except for the rewards of obedience and faithfulness to the Lord. Over the years, many pastors asked me to serve in positions of leadership: youth director, women's ministries director, Sunday school teacher, choir director, Sunday school superintendent, director of Christian education, praise and worship leader, small group leader—not necessarily in that order. Each position involved enlarging my abilities and my borders.

Before my freshman year in high school, a desire growing inside me pushed me to pursue a classic college preparatory diploma with classes in Latin. I would, with God's help, go to college. That decision was the beginning of my first real stretch of faith. I had no savings set aside for college; my parents could usually make ends meet, but that was about all. I had no trust fund set aside by grandparents. I had no imaginable financial help for college, except, possibly, a scholarship. So I worked harder than ever and kept my grades as high as possible. And I asked God to make a way where there seemed to be no way. I didn't realize it at the time, and no one told me, but I was practicing living by faith; I was walking by faith and not by sight. I was stretching.

By that time, I was not sure whether I wanted to be a nurse or a teacher or a journalist. As a sophomore, I was surprised when the teacher/sponsor recruited me to the journalism class and the high school newspaper staff. It was then that I decided I liked writing and reporting but was not cut out to be "pushy" as I labeled the few female news reporters on television in those days. So I read all the novels about Cherry Ames, nurse, that I could find. And I delighted in the memories of being asked to "teach" first and second graders in my elementary school for part of a school day.

Much to my surprise, when it was time to graduate from high school, a double blessing presented possibilities to me. Two scholarships were offered: one at a woman's college in Virginia, a very prestigious place with a highly marketable degree; the other, a teacher scholarship from the State of West Virginia, which provided money for four years of college with a major in education. The latter came with a requirement. I had to teach one year in West Virginia schools for each year I accepted scholarship payments.

My heart wanted to choose the women's college. My head declared it was not possible. I can't remember asking the Lord if He had a choice for me. Even with a liberal scholarship to the women's college, the cost would still have been so great that I could see no way to afford it. (Student loans were unheard of at that time.) Perhaps my faith and my reason collided. So I chose to go to Marshall University, a state school, in spite of its reputation in those days as a "party school." With no interstate highways then, it was approximately 125 miles from home by bus. Dropping the possibility of nursing as a career, I reasoned that I could study to teach English and possibly still become a journalist. The teacher scholarship would pay the way. Never did it occur to me that I would not live in West Virginia long enough to pay off the scholarship.

The spring of high school graduation brought with it a health challenge. The last week and a half of school I spent in bed with what I think was called the Asiatic flu or the Hong Kong flu. Whatever it was called (my recall system is just not what it used to be), that flu made me so ill that I was sure I would die. Mom and Dad may have thought so too. For a full week, I could neither eat nor drink. Even the smell of food made me sick. Sips of water came back up almost immediately. Nothing would stay on my stomach. A community doctor who did house calls came to see me. I never knew what he said to Mom about my condition. Fever ravaged my body, and I actually wanted to die to get out of my misery. However, after five or six days of the illness and much prayer, someone exercised faith. Death would not claim me. The Lord had plans for my life, and I began to mend.

Several pounds lighter and wearing clothing that hung on my thinner frame, I began to be well just in time to wobble through the practice processional and recessional for our baccalaureate service. By graduation time a few days later, I had regained strength enough to enjoy my part in helping to write and produce the graduation ceremony. Traditionally, the high honor graduates enjoyed that honor. By God's grace, my teachers excused me from the final exams administered during the week I was ill and absent from school. God was merciful again.

A few days after graduation, my great aunt called me with a proposition. She wanted to arrange a blind date with the son of her friend, someone that my mother and grandmother also knew but I had never met. I was not quite over getting dumped almost a year earlier by someone I had dated briefly and adored—someone older than I and a lot wiser, someone who was ready to settle down with a wife. I knew I needed to put that experience behind me. With a bit of trepidation born of one previous blind-date experience, I said yes. Surely it would not be so bad since my family knew him and his parents.

Little did I know how that one date would impact my life.

One blind date in June led to other dates throughout the summer. It turned out that James Duncan, the son of the man my great aunt was dating, was at home on leave. A sailor in the United States Navy, James had been burned badly in an explosion on board the *USS Randolph*. Most of his burns were healing nicely, but he had to avoid the sun for several more weeks and wear long sleeves that summer. That was a small price to pay for his life. The explosion had left his co-worker with third degree burns over most of his body. A professed atheist prior to that time, the co-worker had lived long enough and was lucid enough to ask the chaplain to tell his mother he was not really an atheist. He died only a few hours afterward.

When I learned that James was not born again, I had moments of remembering God's Word that advises not to be "unequally yoked with unbelievers" (2 Corinthians 6:14). But dating was not getting married. It was just dating—and maybe just one time. Or so the voice on my shoulder whispered in my ear. Besides, I was on my way to college in a few weeks. I listened.

You can guess the rest of the story. We dated during the summer when he was on leave. When it was time to report to Marshall for my freshman year, we agreed, at his suggestion, to date other people. That plan lasted exactly two weeks. I was not interested in dating anyone else. He said he was not either. So, we embarked on a dating relationship that we had to carry out long distance.

The young sailor whose family had always called James because their father insisted he would not be Jim, was stationed in Norfolk, Virginia, more than five hundred miles from Marshall. He had no car. I had no car. He usually hitchhiked about four hundred miles to his dad's house, and I had to find a ride home to my parents' home about two-and-a-half hours from Marshall. Then, he could borrow his dad's car and drive the three miles to see me. Fortunately, we were able to see each other once or twice a month until his ship returned to the Mediterranean to cruise for six to eight months.

With these decisions, James (whom I dared to call Jim) and I began a relationship that culminated in marriage a few months later while he was still in the US Navy and I was in college. Once he and I became serious about each other, he became the motivation for finishing college in a hurry. I remember the night he asked me to marry him; we had dated for a little over a year. He had still not given his heart to the Lord, but I had allowed the "just one date" to turn into a love story. I did not even think to wait for him to make the decision to follow Christ; we went home from our date to tell Mom and Dad. By the time we got there, they were both in bed. Jim didn't want to wait until the next day; I did. He wanted to ask Dad's permission to marry his firstborn (maybe before he lost his nerve). He won. We knocked at the curtain-covered doorway of their bedroom and asked if we could come in. Surprisingly to us (and thankfully), both parents were awake. I ignored the still, small voice reminding me that we would be "unequally yoked."

Mom looked happy at our news. Dad did not. Right in front of the man I had come to love, he reminded me of the popular legend that sailors are known for having a girl in every port. Worse than that, he reminded me, he had put out hard-earned money for me to start college. I was barely into my second year. He wanted me to finish. I assured him that I had every intention to finish. Jim assured him that he had every intention that I finish. Very reluctantly, Dad agreed that we could marry. With two sighs of relief, we left my parents to whatever emotions gripped them at the beginning of their night's unrest. With restrained exuberance and little time for listening to the voice of God about our plans, we went forward with our strategies for a rather unremarkable winter wedding on a supremely tight budget.

Today I attend elaborate and expensive weddings that send brides-to-be and their families into stress and high blood pressure and enormous debt. Expensive gowns, lots of attendants to be clothed, venues to be arranged, food to be ordered, honeymoons to be planned, homes or apartments to be secured and furnished. Their lists and their costs are unbelievable when I think of mine and Jim's wedding.

With no real budget, we robbed Peter to pay Paul and began planning our wedding. Rather, Jim left the robbing and planning to Mom and me while he escaped back to his ship. Through the Thanksgiving and Christmas breaks, Mom and I sewed a wedding dress, and Mom designed a dress for my oldest sister, my one attendant. I also fed my imagination with pictures of spectacular wedding possibilities.

Between Thanksgiving and Christmas break, I read bride's magazines and dreamed of romantic honeymoons in the Poconos or on some warm beach in the South. I spent hours admiring and wishing for a dreamy long dress. Always wanting to learn and conform to social rules, I looked to etiquette according to Emily Post and other rule makers and chose to make a short dress considered appropriate for the afternoon wedding. (I've noted that brides of all social classes pretty much flaunt such rules today.) It was also cheaper to make. Finally, I felt blessed just to have a special dress, one that I had essentially sewed with a little help from my harried but loving mother with four other daughters to think of.

My pastor by this time was a young man with a wife. Grandma had moved to another church pretty far away from her home. Pastor James was not yet bonded, so he could not perform the ceremony. Our little country church was in dire need of repairs and paint. My family could not afford wedding expenses and church décor, so we went to a larger church that was already beautifully furnished and talked with the minister. A daughter of one of Mom and Dad's friends had recently been married there. The minister allowed us to use the church with no charge, and he would perform the ceremony—but only after a session of marriage counseling. We breathed a sigh of relief. Things were falling into place. Without time or money to order, address, and mail invitations, we invited only our family and close friends by phone and published a newspaper announcement inviting other interested friends.

I started my wedding dress during Christmas break; Mom finished it for me and made my oldest sister's dress. She would be my only attendant. We had a reception in Mom and Dad's small eat-in kitchen: a beautiful but small cake, some punch, nuts, and candies along with wedding themed napkins, plates, and cups. We did not register for elaborate place settings of china and silver and glassware and other gifts brides love to receive. We did not even register for necessities and the mundane things couples need when they "set up housekeeping." Gift cards had not yet been invented. We had no storage solution in my family's small house, and Jim and I had not yet rented an apartment. We were poor as church mice, but we had love. We were surrounded by a loving biological family and a church family who loved us. We loved each other.

And so it happened. It was a cold day in January with ice on the highways and sidewalks and nearly two feet of snow on the ground. By dark, we were on our way to Georgia, our honeymoon trip. Not quite the trip I had dreamed of. We spent most of our honeymoon in Dad Duncan's mobile home in a quiet little town south of Atlanta while he continued his visit in West Virginia. We were two moon-struck young people so consumed with ourselves that we didn't even call home to assure worried parents that we had navigated treacherous highways and arrived safely. Once again, God heard my mom's and my grandmother's prayers. We enjoyed God's protection and returned to a much-deserved tongue lashing a little less than a week later.

After that week together, my new husband went back to his ship in Norfolk, and I went back to my college dorm for the remainder of the school year. After all, he would be gone for six full months, if not longer. Yes, the idea is still very awkward, and I felt supremely out of place, but the dorm room and the meals in the cafeteria were already paid up through the end of the year. Awkward would have to work.

One weekend later, Jim called the hall phone in my dorm. (We had not even heard of cell phones in those days.) It was already curfew time, but he wanted me to meet him in Charleston, about an hour's drive away by car and who knows how much longer by bus. I needed to sneak out of the dorm even though I was married; I feared the dorm mother would not give me permission. He had another weekend before his ship deployed, so he had already left Norfolk and was on his way to me. To save travel time, I needed to meet him in the bus station in Charleston. With fear and trepidation, I said I would meet him. I had no idea how I would manage that rendezvous since I had no car. We had decided we could not pay for the car he had bought from his dad, so we had given it back to him.

The bus would have to work, and it did. My roommate helped me to escape from the dorm, and I caught the first available bus on a street corner a short walk from the dorm. My parents would have had a stroke if they had known that their daughter, still a teenager, was wondering around on the streets of Huntington at almost 11:30 at night. Then she would wait, unchaperoned, in a bus station for her sailor husband to show up some time in the early morning hours. Even though we had a marriage certificate and a ceremony behind us, I felt there was something unseemly about what we were doing. At that time, I was afraid those strangers at the bus station and at the hotel we checked into would think I was a prostitute. Years later, I chuckle about the escapade and tuck it into my memory bank of favorite times in my life.

Today, by God's grace, we have celebrated more than fifty years of marriage. Even though Jim was not committed to serving God when we started dating, he was reared in a Christian home. His dad had preached and pastored a church for several years. His mother, deceased long before we started dating, was known far and wide as a loving, godly woman. My mother and my grandmother had loved her, so I salved my conscience about loving her son and being "unequally yoked" with an unbeliever (2 Corinthians 6:14). We probably should have run the other way, but we didn't. We married without even talking about the important things we should have considered: How would we handle our money? What did we know about living on a budget? Would we have children? If so, how many? What church would we attend, if any? And many other things pertaining to our future together.

Again, God was forgiving and merciful. James gave his heart to God shortly after our first son was born. We have thanked God over and over for his mercy to both of us.

Chapter 11

GROWING IN
SEVERAL DIRECTIONS

Faith by itself isn't enough.
Unless it produces good deeds,
it is dead and useless.
–James 2:17 (NLT)

———

With a strong desire born of being married and keeping my promise to Dad, I decided to earn my degree in a hurry. By going to summer school, I was able to finish the requirements just two years later. So, in January, five days after finishing undergraduate work at Marshall, I went to work at West Technical High School in Cleveland, Ohio, as an English teacher. (It was an unexplainable but delightful coincidence that James had finished high school and earned his diploma from the evening division of that very high school.) That job began the next challenge.

Teaching high school English can stretch a wife and mother. And a husband, as it turned out. The lesson preparation, the paper grading, the research for something interesting and relevant to present to teens, some curious, some intellectual, most totally oblivious to the need to learn not to split an infinitive or leave a participle dangling — all of this almost overwhelmed me. Thank God for a thoughtful, loving husband who helped me grade the papers that required multiple choice or fill-in-the-blank answers. His sacrifice left me time to assess the essays of 180 students in my first semester of six classes. Sometimes we both stayed up until well after midnight trying just to keep me ahead of the eight ball.

And then the day came; the challenging twelve-hour days of work including four or five hours a day of paper grading and lesson planning during the week came to a screeching halt. Pregnancy happened. In those days, in my school district, I was required to stop teaching just as soon as I began to look pregnant. That was a pretty common requirement of school systems then. So I reluctantly tendered my resignation to coincide with Christmas break. I did not request pregnancy leave; no such thing was available to me at that time.

A few short months later, the two of us became three, and a baby boy turned our lives upside down. As the oldest of five girls, I had had my share of looking after children. I was not afraid of them, but I found out the hard way just how different life is after your own baby joins the scene. It's one thing to help diaper and feed a baby sibling. At night I could go to sleep and let Mom or Dad take on the sleeplessness of nights with hungry or colicky babies. Where were Mom and Dad when I needed them? More than 350 miles away. No sisters to babysit for us; no relatives to support us with encouraging words.

What would we have done without a loving church family? Filled with the love of God and blessed with the heart of servants, they rallied to the occasion. They gave us a wonderful shower and blessed us, not only with much-needed clothing and a diaper service subscription, but also new nursery furniture. They even offered to babysit from time to time. It may have been more than we could have hoped for from our biological family. In retrospect, stretching into the role of mom and dad was not nearly as laborious as I thought it might be.

After we had our first child, that wonderful husband and dad with an unselfish heart began to be required to work long hours and often seven days a week at his job. He stretched in one direction; I stretched in another. The women with servants' hearts from my church became my spiritual support system. They practiced what they found in Scripture about serving one another in love (Galatians 5:13). I thrived in their love and that of my husband and new baby in spite of the challenges.

Whatever their age, boys test parents. We eventually had two. (I can't speak about the challenges of rearing girls even though I grew up with four sisters. We never had a girl of our own until our first granddaughter joined the family.) By the time our second child was born nearly three years after the first, we had moved to Georgia. The decision to move was not an easy one. We dearly loved our church family in Ohio. The pastor's daughters were close to our age, and the whole family had accepted us and treated us like family. We had many other good friends close to our age there, friends with whom we had an active social life. By this time, I was involved in church ministry as director of the youth program and had begun to sing in the community choir. Jim was enjoying the benefits of a good-paying job with General Motors after working for Ford and the IBEW briefly.

So why did we move? Only because *God called us enlarge our borders,* this time to another state. Jim's brother and sisters and their families lived in Georgia, just south of Atlanta. We had visited there, and I was learning to love them. Soon after we became pregnant with our second child, we both found ourselves in tears every time we talked about his family members and the fact that none of them were living for the Lord. Their children were not learning about Jesus. They rarely, if ever, went to church. It seemed to us that God was calling us to minister to them. We didn't even question Him about how that ministry might look. We simply made plans to leave our good life in Ohio.

Since Jim worked for General Motors in Ohio, we reasoned that he could probably get a job at the GM plant in Atlanta. It was located near the area where his family lived. But we had no assurance, no promise of a job, and we had no money for a move. We just borrowed money from a brother-in-law and moved by faith. Had we been a few years older and a bit more worldly wise, we might have missed God's call at that time. Here I was almost five months pregnant. We had to sell our home with more than enough room for two children in Ohio and move into a small apartment in Georgia. We had no income. We didn't even ask where it was coming from. We fully believed God would supply our needs, so we just stretched into what we still believe was God's will for our lives at the time.

— — — — — — — — — — — — — — — —

We had already moved from Huntington, West Virginia, home of Marshall University, my alma mater. Huntington was the place where I wanted to settle down. I had dreamed of earning my master's degree and teaching at Marshall. That was not to happen.

After fulfilling his military obligation, Jim could not find a job there or anywhere near. I prayed. He searched. Nothing was available. He could claim a job at the company he had left to join the military; it was waiting for him in Cleveland. So, he went there. I finished my summer session and another semester at Marshall before joining him full-time in Ohio. My loving husband did not complain. Instead, we conducted a long distance marriage for six months. Long bus rides for me or long car trips on weekends for him had to suffice. We managed.

Then we made the first move of our short married life. When I finished my last semester in early January, snow and ice covered the ground and the highways in Ohio and West Virginia. Jim worked his eight-hour shift in Ohio and drove the usual five- or six-hour trip in about seven hours. Out of necessity, we emptied the neatly packed boxes I had ready and literally stuffed most of my belongings in the car. We set out for West 83rd Street in Cleveland. As we entered Ohio, we noted a temperature of 19 degrees below zero on a building we passed.

Along the way, we had to stop for gas and a bathroom break. The thermometer on the gas station showed 24 degrees below zero. That was the first open station we had seen in miles, and it was hours until opening time in the morning. A bathroom accessed from an outside door was located in the same building as the station. Thick icicles clung to the edge of the roof just above the bathroom door, and ice sealed the frame. The door was firmly stuck. When we finally, by brute strength, forced the door open, I discovered that the water in the toilet was frozen; still, it would have to suffice. Even the water in the wash basin pipes had frozen so I couldn't wash my hands. My insides shook from the cold. That cold night is something I'll never forget.

The rest of the trip was uneventful. I couldn't keep my eyes open. I worried about Jim, who had worked all day and was, as it appeared, about to drive all night. Not enough, though, to keep me fully awake. With God watching over us and with the good sense of most other drivers to stay off the highways, we made it across long miles of road-ways with icy patches and deep snow piles on the sides of the roads to our furnished apartment without incident. We were home just in time to unload the car that had the look of Sanford and Son about it so Jim could go to work.

Stopping only to wash his face and hands and grab a sandwich to eat on the way, Jim left for work. I tried to dissuade him. He'd already been up twenty-four hours and now planned to work for eight hours without sleeping. He insisted on going to work. His desire to take care of his family financially is something I came to admire and appreciate early in our marriage. I prayed for him and did the sensible thing. I went to bed.

Moving by Faith

So we made the second major move of our short married life, and I gave birth to our second baby boy four months later. By this time, we had settled into a church that accepted us and made us feel part of the church family. I discovered that two boys required much more time and supervision than I ever thought possible. Not wanting to have someone else influence their earliest years, I found myself happy to take time from a professional job to be a stay-at-home mom and homemaker. It was the right thing for me to do. After being promised a job at General Motors in two or three months after our move, Jim accepted a position with Nabisco for the interim. It did not pay as well as the GM job, but it put food on the table and paid our bills. Most of them. Most of the time.

One day when our second child, Lynn, (He eventually decided he liked his first name Zachary better and wanted to be called Zach; we honored his choice.) was just a few months old, we found ourselves in a bit of a financial bind. We had only two bottles of formula left, and no money to buy any more. It was early in the day and three days yet to payday. Jim was working the second shift at Nabisco. When he got up that day, we talked about how we might handle the emergency. Since the move to Georgia, we were over 500 miles from my mom and dad. We had no ability to get quick help there. He suggested we might borrow money from his sister or her husband, the one who had loaned money for our move.

Almost immediately, he revoked that suggestion as he voiced his thinking. I don't remember his exact words, but they were something like this: "We can't do that. We've come here to help my family to know and trust the Lord. What kind of example will it be for me to have to borrow money again?"

I don't remember which of us suggested it, but we got on our knees in our living room that afternoon and petitioned God to provide. We determined to trust him. As we prayed, we could hear the soft shuffle of mail dropping onto the floor from the mail drop in our front door. We continued to pray until we felt that we had finished. Then we checked the mail.

We must have been a bit like the church members who had gathered to pray for Peter to be released from jail. Do you remember the story? It's told in Acts 12.

Herod had killed the apostle James, brother of John, and put Peter in prison and charged four quaternions (squads of four soldiers each) with guarding him. Herod intended to bring him out and deliver him to the people after Easter. Meanwhile the church prayed for him without ceasing.

One night, while Peter, bound in chains, slept between two soldiers, the angel of God came to him and told him to get up quickly and get dressed. Waking up from a deep sleep, he could have rubbed his eyes and wondered if he was hallucinating. He could have questioned, "Who are you? What are you doing here?" He could have turned over and gone back to sleep again. He did none of that. He got up quickly. When he did, his chains fell off, he walked past all the guards, and the outside door of the prison opened of its own accord. God was at work. Peter didn't question the angel's instructions. He didn't question the miraculous walk past the guards and the open door. Instead, he simply followed. By the time Peter and the angel had passed through the prison gates and one street, the angel disappeared. Peter was now on his own.

Up to this time, Peter moved, maybe as if in a daze. He thought he might be having a vision. The Bible says he came to himself, realized he was free, and went to the home of Mary, the mother of John Mark. It was there that many people were praying for him. He knocked at the door of the gate. The girl who answered the door didn't even open it to let him come in. She was so surprised that she ran to tell the people that he was outside. Like many believers, they prayed for Peter's release, seemingly as if they didn't believe God would answer.

God was at work even while Peter slept. He was at work while the people prayed. He answered their prayers that, given their lack of belief that Peter was at the gate, must have been accompanied with little faith. God showed Himself faithful. Without any help from human agency, He freed Peter from his shackles and from the well-guarded prison.

I have discovered that what God did for Peter, He'll do for you. You simply have to trust Him. You can be so free of worry and frustration that you can lie down and sleep while your situation looks bleak to human eyes. You can go free from the prison of addiction. You can escape the prisons of indecision, illness, or a poverty mentality. You can be free of depression, panic attacks, and other mental anguish. He promised that what we ask in faith, whatever we ask and believe that we receive, we shall have (Mark 11:24). We *shall* have. Not maybe. Not if we prove good enough. Not if we mind our p's and q's. *If we believe!*

Jim and I have seen God's faithfulness many times in our lives. We saw it the day we needed money for our baby's formula. God was at work even before we prayed. Much to my surprise and Jim's, one letter in that mail drop came from an employer where Jim had worked briefly two years before. It had the correct address on the envelope. Inside the envelope was a check for $57 and change. The enclosed letter identified the check as a bonus he had earned during the time he had worked there. We could purchase the necessary formula and other things we needed until payday at the end of the week.

God showed Himself faithful again. Even today, and almost every day, I have to remind myself that His Word is truth. What He says, He will do. He had been planning for our needs all the time. He saw to it that the check came just in time for us to realize an answered prayer. He will do the same for you. As Jesus said to His disciples, "Whatever things you ask for in prayer [in accordance with God's will], believe [with confident trust] that you *have received* them, and they will be given to you." (Mark 11:24 AMP; emphasis added)

Note that the Lord said the key to receiving is to believe that you have already received your request before you pray. That day we believed, and we received. It was one of many times we received God's direct intervention as a result of our prayer. So we praised God, and life continued somewhat uneventfully for a time.

Facing Greater Challenges

In the middle of life as usual and waiting for Jim's better job to open, we had a call from a friend many miles away. She needed help. The help involved our taking in a teenaged girl whose family member had molested her. At the time, we had only a two- bedroom apartment, but we couldn't say no. Our baby was in a crib; Larry, his older brother, just barely three years old, was in a twin bed. Another twin bed was in the room with the boys. We found room. She could stay there. God was at work. It was as if He was saying to us, "Enlarge your borders. You can do it. I am with you. My grace is sufficient."

Whew! We were young and so inexperienced. What did we have to offer a hurting young lady who had not had any counseling to help her deal with the tragic circumstances of her life? We had ignorance. We had lack of experience. We had indecision. But we had what might matter in the long run. We had love. We knew how to pray. We were learning how to trust God. And we had just experienced the marvelous deliverance from lack. Trusting that anything else we needed would be supplied, we invited her to come and stay indefinitely.

Today, I can't remember how long she stayed. It was several months, maybe a year. She tended to be reclusive. Many years later, I know enough to understand why. At the time, I didn't. She loved our boys and was tender and caring with them, but she was so sad most of the time. With a few words here and there she let us know that she missed her mother and brothers. She missed her church. She even missed the one who had betrayed her trust. We prayed fervently for this hurting child of God. We gave her all the love she would allow us to give. We took her to church and encouraged her to know that God loved her then and loved her still. We left her in the hands of her heavenly Father believing that He could do for her what we could not.

After several months, our precious girl called her mother and went home: back to the place where she could have been in danger again, back to her mom and her siblings. I can only imagine her fears and her questions. She never spoke one word of them to me before or after she went home. Life went on, and we lost touch. Eventually, we learned from a family member that she had married and had children of her own. But members of her extended family said she had lost her child-like faith in God. Little wonder.

Another time, several years later, when the boys were teens, God put another young woman in our path. This one was homeless. We met her at church. She told us that her husband had left her after their baby died of SIDS (sudden infant death syndrome); we called it crib death. Honestly, we were not convinced, but we could help. Our church paid for two nights in a motel and a few meals. Somehow she made it to the next service. Afterwards, we talked with her. She was almost overcome with grief and still had no prospects for a job. We were hooked.

We took this young woman, whom I'll call Juanita, and her few meager belongings home with us. We didn't even think of the possible dangers of a strange girl in the home with our two sons, who, by this time, were in their teens. Boys, had we only stopped to think, who had raging hormones. We didn't give one thought to the possibility that she might be on drugs (she wasn't) or that she might get angry and try to kill all of us. (Obviously, she didn't.) Or that her ex-husband might come out and torch the house. We simply trusted God. Thankfully, He was faithful. He didn't let us down.

As Juanita lived with us, ate with us, played with us, and went to church with us, we learned some disconcerting things about her life. If my memory serves me, she had given birth to two children in three years. Both had died. She said she feared that her estranged husband had killed their first as well as their second child. Autopsies had concluded that SIDS was the reason for the death of both babies, but Juanita was not convinced. She constantly expressed fear for her life. We thought she was just distraught and overcome with grief. We tried to console her with Scripture and the love that we had to offer and the love that God offered. She knelt at the church altar with us, seeking solace, seeking peace of mind, and seeking a love that she wasn't sure was there.

At some point she must have told her story in front of the right law enforcement person. After what seemed to be an interminably long time, police investigated the husband thoroughly. As I recall, authorities had the first baby's body exhumed. They found evidence supporting wrongful death. Then the investigators must have put some stock in her suspicion that her husband had something to do with the deaths of both babies. They exhumed the second body. With the possibility of murder in the picture, the criminal investigative services found evidence supporting a second wrongful death. They took Juanita's husband into custody.

Eventually, Juanita's husband was charged, tried, and found guilty of murder in the death of the two babies. Finally, we could understand Juanita's fears and her concerns for her own life. We mourned that we had been able to talk with the ex-husband, but he had not given his heart to Christ. We mourned for the mother who lost her two babies and had, subsequently, lost her faith in a loving God. We mourned that we had not been able to lead her to hope in the Lord. We hope that the seed we planted took root.

Shortly after her husband's conviction, Juanita moved out. By that time, she had a job making minimum wage and tips. She had found another place to stay. Although we tried to keep in touch, she quietly got lost in another life.

———◈———

Back to our boys and their restless mother: the two boys and I busied ourselves playing and learning as quietly as possible during the days when Jim worked nights. We took frequent walks in the neighborhood and spent many days at the pool trying to occupy ourselves outside the small home so he could sleep as much as possible. Trying to keep them out of daycare, I was taking care of our boys. But I was longing to accomplish something worthwhile. Seriously? Seriously!

As a young mother in the heyday of Gloria Steinem and others who preached that women were wasting their time in the home, that women could have a profession to fulfill them and still be good wives and mothers, I was allowing myself to become indoctrinated. I didn't know it then, but I loaned my ear to the whispering serpent, just as Eve did.

Little did I recognize that the best job in the world is that of mother. That God places children in the care of mothers and fathers whose sacred *privilege* it is to train them up in the way they should go so that they will not leave the right way when they are older (Proverbs 22:6). Bringing children into the world is not for wimps. It is not for the wildly careless and irresponsible who think only of themselves and their desires. In an ideal world, parenting would be reserved for those who want children, those who are strong, those who are willing to make a lifetime commitment to loving, instructing, training, and guiding. I was willing to do all that as long as it didn't interfere with my professional goals and aspirations. (Are you grimacing at my naiveté yet?)

Before mothers everywhere unite to tar and feather me, let me assure all working mothers and single parents that I understand your need to be away from the children. God knows, and I understand, that it is necessary for you to clothe their bodies and put bread on their table and a roof over their heads. In an ideal world, you would be able to supervise your own children and nurture them. Unfortunately, we don't live in an ideal world. But I firmly believe that God sees your circumstances and that He will help you to be what you need to be to your children. When you trust your children to Him, when you trust your life plight to Him, when you trust Him to work all things together for your good and theirs (Romans 8:28), He shows up. You can count on Him to meet your needs and those of your family. Like every other provision He has made, you and I have to access these with our faith.

Even while giving our boys the gift of Mom's presence and loving supervision, I felt something was missing. I found myself getting irritable and longing for adult conversation during the day. I joked with friends that my little ones were better served when I was working. Little did I realize what I was giving up when I went back to work. I reasoned that a retired couple in a small house with one other child to care for would give them loving care. Thankfully, they did.

So I sacrificed my children's destiny to be reared by their own mother for my desires. I see that in retrospect. I didn't see the possible long-term consequences of my decision then. I had no idea that one day I would regret my choice, but I gladly took the teaching position offered at Fayette County High School in Fayette County, Georgia. And I marveled at another peculiar coincidence. My dad had lived in Fayette County, West Virginia, and had gone to Fayette County High School.

Trying to Do It All

After several years of learning to teach and practicing my profession I found myself in need of another challenge, I stretched toward a new educational goal. My inspiration was a woman I worked with and admired. As a single mom of teenaged boys, she found time to be a good teacher while she pursued a master's degree. I thought if she could do it, so could I. At least, I reasoned, I have a husband who would help. So I decided I could do it all and not become like her. With God's help and encouragement from my husband, I dived into the deep end of the pool known as graduate school. There I was: working full time while pursuing a graduate degree part time. I determined to be a good wife, mother, homemaker, teacher, and youth director at a small suburban church. I believed I could do it all and do it well.

It wasn't until several years later that I learned that the person my inspiration portrayed on the stage called her life was not the same person she was behind the scenes. The challenges of her full and busy life became too much for her, but she could not see that she needed to simplify. She became irrational and eccentric. She was definitely not who I wanted to be. But I persisted. With God's help I would not become like her.

Living hundreds of miles from my family and the natural support they give, I leaned heavily on my hardly-ever-there husband, his baby sister, the baby sitter, and our church family. Again, God provided. With His help I earned a master's degree while working full time. Another goal reached. I had stretched. My reward was a coveted piece of paper, a ticket that would open another door, an entrance for me into the realm of supervision at some future time.

The years passed. Our mission trip to Georgia began, with God's help, to be successful. After persistent encouragement from us, both of Jim's sisters and his sister-in-law began attending church with their children. They gave their hearts to Jesus. They became active, first in the church we attended, and then in churches of their choice. We encouraged their husbands to accept Christ. They put off their decisions until much later in life, but they came to Christ before their deaths. Nieces came to Christ, but nephews procrastinated. Our children were doing well in school and in youth sports activities. They loved going to church and participating in the ministries geared to them. We felt fulfilled. As a family, we were happy.

Then came a time, some six years after we had built the house of our dreams and put down roots with freshly planted trees when God spoke to us again. Our boys were eight and eleven years old. Both Jim and I had lucrative jobs that we enjoyed. We had been blessed with promotions on our jobs. We loved our church and were active in ministry there. Our children were in youth league sports with their school friends. Even though we had a good life, something began to seem amiss. After much prayer and disquiet, we believed we heard the Holy Spirit calling us to another mission field.

At the time, I had sisters who lived in Maryland. Although they had grown up in the same house with me, had gone to the same church, and had given their hearts to God as children, they and their families were away from God. They seemingly had little to no interest in church or the things of God. They were busy living the lifestyles of their choice and letting their children grow up with no religious instruction at all.

We cried for them this time. Was God's voice what we were hearing? I couldn't talk to just anyone about it—not even the supportive women who lovingly gave me direction from time to time. Neither could Jim. We talked with each other. We talked to God—separately and together. I wondered if we were just reaching a point in our lives where we were becoming restless because of the lack of "real" challenge in our lives. We prayed more. Finally, sure that we had heard from God, we made a decision.

Following what we were convinced was God's inspiration and direction, we left the home we had begun to enjoy. We moved to Maryland—away from a church family that we loved, away from the first home we had ever built, away from good jobs, and away from good friends to a different climate, to a different church, and to different work environments and jobs. Fortunately, Jim continued with General Motors. I wasn't sure what I wanted to do, so I decided I was happy spending some time with the sisters I had not been close to since I moved out of my parents' home to go to college. I looked for a job a few months into our move.

After substitute teaching in an elementary school a few times, I became certain that I didn't want to work in public schools in Maryland. So I searched around, somewhat half-heartedly, for work at nearby universities. I had a master's degree and a successful work history both in public school and in a junior college. Surely someone would want me. I prayed for guidance and favor and set out to look for a teaching position in a university setting. I decided to stretch some more.

The head of the English department at Johns' Hopkins University agreed to see me. He chuckled as he dropped his bombshell. The English department had not hired full-time teachers in nine full years and currently did not need anyone—not even part-time instructors in that department. I heard a similar story at the University of Maryland. While I was looking elsewhere, the pastor at the church where we settled laid a scary proposition in my lap. The church had been planning a day-care center with after-school care there for almost a year. They had the facility and were pursuing the appropriate permits and licenses. They needed someone with a college degree to head it.

Plenty of the church members had degrees, but I was the only one with a degree who was not working full time. Pastor Peninger and his wife Martha had done some of the preliminary work. She would have served as director, but she didn't have the degree. Would I please take on the role of director? I put him off again and again. They continued doing what they could and looked to God to provide the need. Finally, seeing that I was unable to find a job I wanted, I agreed at least to think about it. I did not feel it. I did not feel called to it. I had absolutely no training in that area. I loved big kids, high school and college-aged kids and adults, not day-care age. In my heart of hearts, I really did not want to do it, but I couldn't shake an inner voice reminding me of the need.

Yes, something compelled me. I prayed about it, but I was afraid to hear from the Lord. My mind rebelled at the very thought of getting involved in a day-care center. Pastor Peninger persisted. I resisted. Honestly, in retrospect, I now know I was not seeking to fulfill God's will at that time. I wanted to do my thing—whatever that was. Eventually, I caved in to the gentle nudging of the pastor and the Spirit of God, but I gave them (not God, just Pastor and his wife, or so I said) my terms. I really wanted to follow God's plan and be in His will, but I wanted to do it my way.

Finally, I agreed to become temporary director of The Little People Center. I would do everything I could to help get the center to a profitable state. Rather self-righteously, I offered to volunteer all my time and labor until the center opened and enrolled children. I would then take a salary that would barely cover my expenses. Even the full-time teachers would make more money than I did. But before I could open the center, I had to take the state mandated six-week course for day-care workers because my degrees were not in early childhood education. And I had to pay for it myself. Seriously, God? To be brutally honest, I thought this requirement was beneath me.

What a step back. Or so I thought. I wanted to teach college classes. I was ready to teach college classes in Maryland. I had taught part time at a local junior college near my home in Georgia. Here I was in Maryland at the Lord's urging, and I was relegated to organizing and implementing day care. Outside my comfort zone, for sure. After a good bit of wrestling with my thoughts and a long self-examination, I decided I may as well jump into the new assignment with as much enthusiasm and dedication as I could muster. When all was said and done, I couldn't bear to do otherwise. God gave me a nature to do my best in whatever situation I find myself.

I didn't think about it then, but I've since learned that God often calls us to a work for which we are not prepared. He'll prepare us. When He calls us to start over or to engage in a work for which we're overqualified or underqualified, He has a plan. Usually, He wants to teach us something: to lean into Him, to follow the plans He has for us, to do it gracefully and gratefully.

A story in the Bible illustrates what I'm talking about. When God told Gideon (as recorded in Judges 6–8) to lead an attack against the Midianites who had overrun Israel at one time, Gideon raised an army of 32,000 men. After God assessed the situation, He gave the warrior leader instructions to cut the army size down to less than one percent of the original size. He then informed Gideon that He did not want Israel to be able to claim that they had defeated the enemy army in their own strength. Perhaps I needed to relearn not to go in my own strength and ability.

After about six months, the center showed a profit. The Lord provided a contract with a nearby hospital administrator for space for their employees' children. I couldn't even take credit for that success; Pastor negotiated it. The hospital would pay for twenty children whether the spaces were filled or not. The agreement was a savings to them. They wouldn't have to configure a facility, hire a staff, and pay benefits. It was a blessing to the church. God was definitely blessing our efforts, but I thought I needed a real paycheck. (I admitted to myself that I also needed a job with more status. I didn't tell anyone else that, not even my husband. Pride was trying to take hold of me.)

Even though I was not doing the work I thought I should be doing, I found myself challenged on a different level. I was learning to obey the Lord. I was learning patience. Much to my surprise, I was also learning to love little children and their parents. My hardest lesson came about three months into the operation.

Before The Little People Center opened, the pastor, the board, and I agreed that the center would give first preference to church members who wanted to work and were qualified. One of the teachers, Mrs. X, was a member of the church; she really wanted a job. With well-behaved children of her own and basic qualifications, she seemed to be acceptable. I figured her lack of experience would not be a hindrance because she appeared to be a good mother and wife, and she had been faithful in church attendance and service in the children's ministry. She and other church members took the requisite coursework and helped open the day care center. She had good attendance, prepared lessons, and reasonable classroom management skills, but her classes lacked energy and creativity. Though not stellar, her performance was acceptable.

As the center grew, it became necessary to hire those who were not members of the church. Soon we needed to expand the number of classes. I hired a well-qualified young teacher who had an educational advantage and some experience. She was dynamite in the classroom: energetic, creative, well-prepared, interested, and interesting. I was thankful for her. That she was not a member of the church did not seem to be an issue. However, it was not long until Mrs. X began to find fault with the new hire. She began to bring accusations against her "rival." I believed her, so my investigations were a bit half-hearted. I met with the younger teacher, talked with her, and heard her deny the accusations. But, unfortunately for me, I gave more credence to Mrs. X's story because she was a church member. After a second accusation, I let Miss Y go, telling her it seemed that she was not a good fit for the job.

Much to my chagrin, I discovered after a few weeks that Mrs. X had manufactured some and embellished other tales she told me. I was mortified that a very costly lesson, at least for two of us, had presented itself during my watch. I learned that I can't always trust the professing Christian to be truthful; the young teacher learned that even Christian directors of church-supported enterprises cannot be trusted to investigate for the truth of the matters that concern their employees. Today I shudder at my decision and the impact it must have had on the younger woman.

After a few months, with the pastor's blessing, I began to take time to look for a different job. Sometime later, after I had finished my term as director of the child care center, nearby Prince George's Community College offered me a part-time position teaching Composition 101. That job salved my ego. Carefully, I considered the possibility of working a full-time and a part-time job. I reasoned that my husband's job at GM started early in the morning and ended early enough in the day that our boys would be well-supervised if my days grew long. Did I say, "If"? Inevitably, they did. I accepted the offer, only two evenings a week, with Jim's blessing, and continued to look for full-time work.

I tried my best to avoid going to Washington, DC, some twenty-five miles away from where we eventually bought a home, but that must have been where God wanted me. I applied for and was interviewed for editing jobs closer to home. The businesses hired someone else. At long last, the American Chemical Society, a nonprofit in the heart of Washington and across the street from the Russian Embassy, offered two different jobs. I had to wait about a week after the HR director gave her go-ahead to interview with the potential bosses. Both were men. Both were in Hawaii at the society's annual conference. An airline strike hindered their return to the mainland for a few days. I chomped at the bit while winter set in with a vengeance.

Finally, both of them returned. They interviewed me. I interviewed them. One of them offered me a job before I had interviewed with the second one. With a bit of fear and trembling, I waited. I told the department head who offered that I would like to wait until I heard from the division head. He graciously agreed. Finally, the division head offered me the job in his office. Heady experience! Two job offers ended months of drought.

After some thought and prayer, I took the job as the administrative assistant to the Director of the Books and Journals Division of the American Chemical Society. I was an English major surrounded by chemistry majors. Interesting? For sure. Challenging? Absolutely. And I again became somewhat of a peon, but I had a decent paycheck. It was as good as the one I had left behind in Georgia.

No longer was I the manager of my own team, though. I had been accustomed to shepherding the English department while commanding my classroom, making decisions, giving directions, meeting with parents and students, meeting with counselors and principal, having my experience and my words count. Then, at the day-care center, I was pretty much in charge. I interviewed and recommended workers for hire to the board, made schedules, interviewed with parents, interacted with teachers and students, supervised the staff, planned menus, and generally was Jill of all trades.

This was a new ballgame with a new coach and a new manager. Would I get kicked off the team? Not if I could help it. Not if the Lord would help me. I prayed for His help. He answered with unexpected blessings and favor. Within three months my salary had increased by almost seventy percent. I liked the people I worked with. I felt appreciated, but I was restless, unfilled. I felt prepared to take on greater responsibility. It was not offered. To this day, I'm not sure why the Lord saw fit to open a job for me there. Perhaps my patience needed a workout.

And I continued the part-time teaching job. Both of my jobs lasted until I resigned. Jim and I reached a time when we felt that the Lord was finished with us in Maryland. Our boys were bombarded constantly with temptation to drugs. My husband hated city life. We were surrounded by city in every direction within a fifty-mile radius. He was ready to leave long before I was.

I became willing to leave, but we were entrenched in church work. I was leading the worship team and directing state youth camps. Jim had a small group made up of teenagers, mostly boys, whom he loved and poured his life into. We both were busy with state youth camps and retreats. God was enlarging our borders and stretching us into ministry we had never dreamed of doing. Our ministry expanded to areas across the state and the nation with involvement in men's and women's conferences, national and international women's conferences, and marriage conferences we eventually helped to organize and conduct. We stretched our leadership training and teaching into the hotel industry.

I loved it all. I was enjoying living close to this part of my family for the first time in more than thirteen years. One sister and her family had moved back to West Virginia by that time. Two sisters were still there in Maryland. Both of them had started going to church while we were there. Both had begun to live God-first lives. Their children were finally in church and faithful. One was a single mom who struggled to meet the needs of her family. The other had not worked since the birth of her only child. Her husband would listen to us talk about God's love, but he would not accept Christ as his Savior and Lord. We continued to love him and live the godly example before him as best as we knew how.

After a little more than four years there, it seemed that we had accomplished what we went there to do. Our boys were active in their children's and youth groups; the older one loved youth camp. We were happy as a family, but our boys were constantly hounded with temptations: drugs, disobedience to parents, and adventures into areas outside our comfort zone. Their schools also served the nearby army base, which filled and emptied with young people who were constantly coming and leaving. For most of them, their parents came to the area temporarily with pending military assignments and left soon. Many of their classmates were unruly and worldly—far more knowledgeable about the "carnal" life than I wanted our boys to be at their ages. I didn't want them to stretch in that direction. I finally agreed to go back to Georgia.

God gave us the go-ahead. Both boys and I moved in time to start the new school year. Jim had to work out the year before his transfer would be official. We reasoned that the end of August until Christmas would not be that long. We could do it, and we did.

Longing to fulfill another dream, I had started work on a PhD degree in English literature while we were living in Maryland. By the time we moved back to Georgia a couple of years later, I knew that was not the area of my greatest interest. Without my knowledge, the Lord seemed to be setting the stage for me to get into administration in public schools. It was something I had never before aspired to do. However, as the doors opened, I stepped in. Each new position provided just the challenge I needed personally. My husband moved into management. Our lives became ever more challenging. Our time with the Lord in spiritual development took a back seat to ever-pressing "busyness."

Time management and organization became of paramount importance to me. The boys became teenagers. Learning to drive, playing sports, and learning to live and to feel right in their skin consumed their lives. Jim and I tried to provide the appropriate supervision and care while allowing them to spread their wings. We learned that, contrary to popular opinion, teens require more active parental supervision than small babies. I could teach a workshop on that topic. Maybe another time.

Chapter 12

REACHING HIGHER

And whatsoever ye do in word or deed,
do all in the name of the Lord Jesus.
–Colossians 3:17

———◆———

B ack at the church we had left four years before, we were quickly drafted into active ministry again. Soon I found myself teaching a weekly Bible study and leading worship. Those activities definitely stretch believers—if they do it right. If that's what God calls them to do. I really felt those ministry opportunities were my calling. Strangely, I had little formal training in either field.

I've joked that I was born with music in my blood. Everyone in my family had some musical ability. My mother's mother was summarily dismissed from (I loved calling it "kicked out of") piano lessons as a child. She found her music by ear and disregarded the music lesson she was supposed to practice. Dad's dad could chord an organ. My dad sang, taught himself to play mandolin and harmonica, and had a huge record collection he shared with his girls. Mom sang at church and at the house as she worked.

Mom and Dad and the grandparents passed on their interests in and love for music to my siblings and me. I have always loved to sing and could harmonize as a little girl. All of my sisters can sing. As young people we didn't sing as much by note (music as written) as we did by "let'er." One musician tried to help. He came to the church to teach music by what I think was called shape note and left the church disappointed. He said all we wanted to do was just open up and "let'er fly." We've come a bit of a distance since then.

Rita plays piano and keyboard by ear. A part of the worship team, she's a frequent soloist in her church. Carol declares she can't sing, but I listen to her sometimes when we're in church together. She can sing. Linda is an anointed worship leader. Kathy, our baby sister, was in band, learned to play piano, and became the church pianist. She and her husband have continued to learn and have recorded CDs with lyrics and voices balanced by full orchestras and featuring guitars. Beautiful music. Anything but noise! We still love making a joyful noise to the Lord. By the standards of more highly trained musicians, and the older we get, that may be all it is, just a joyful noise. But all of us have learned that whom the Lord calls, He qualifies if we're willing.

I have loved music of almost every genre. Even today, in a local church that features contemporary music almost exclusively, I can worship as long as I can hear and understand the words of the songs. Unfortunately, my generation, which grew up singing hymns with traditional chords and timing and little to no amplification, sometimes cannot listen through loud music, which often overwhelms the lyrics.

My only formal training in music was six months of piano lessons at the age of twelve and two years of chorus in high school. My training in the Bible consisted of personal study with a concordance and formal classes that led to certification as a Bible teacher in my church denomination. But I fully believed then and still believe today that whom He calls, He qualifies. I trusted Him, but I worked hard to improve my skills and my knowledge in music. Teaching Sunday school was also in my blood from the age of twelve when I eagerly accepted my first vacation Bible school class. I jumped at that chance and have never looked back.

So, I went back to work in the local church. I taught English classes in high school and a nearby university during the week. Then I filled Sunday morning with teaching and leading worship at church, along with fulfilling my roles as wife, mother, homemaker, professional, and student. From this vantage point many years later, I ask myself, "Did I fulfill all of my assignments with excellence? Did my preparation for the Lord's work honor Him?" Hindsight may or may not tell the true story. Looking back, I can't see how my offering to the Lord was as excellent as it could have been if I had not been involved in so many things. I can see now I probably struggled in too many directions. As I reflect on my life, I hope I did my best within the busy time frame. I was still trying to please a God whose grace I really didn't yet know.

I was also doing every job in the church that I could do in an effort to "earn" His approval and to "earn" my way to heaven. I was trying to "be good" so as to "get good." And that didn't seem to be enough.

Still straining forward and trying to gain status, I thought full-time work and part-time ministry weren't enough. With my husband's blessing and encouragement, I stretched off into graduate school for a third time. Adding women's conferences, conferences and workshops on marriage, as well as professional conferences to my speaking agenda, I found time somewhere to continue to seek degrees. I've always loved the challenge of learning (and intend to be a lifelong learner). I was stretching, growing. In my mind, it was not only necessary but profitable to stretch. Some of it I did from my knees, an appropriate place from which to expand life's interests and accomplishments.

Please understand that I don't see myself as a scholar. Not by a long shot. I love to learn just for the sake of learning, but I've never aspired to add to the world's information. I simply am curious (my husband says I'm nosy) and love to find answers to my questions. The most I've hoped to do is to achieve the goals of graduate degrees and find the doors those degrees offer to open. For a coal miner's daughter, that was a heady thought. First a master's degree. Done! Then a master's add-on in leadership. Done! Then a specialist in education degree. Perhaps possible.

Meanwhile, our children married and moved out. GM offered early retirement to Jim, which he accepted, and he moved from corporate work to entrepreneurship. We could afford a modest vacation house. Years of searching for something affordable on a lake within reasonable driving distance from our house and family led to much disappointment. We found terrain stretching almost cliff-like down to the water, boat docks that had been grounded as years of drought dried up the lake, homes appealing to our aesthetics that were miles above our budget. About three years into the search, we struck gold.

We found Lake Oconee, just east of Atlanta. There we bought a small cottage in a shallow cove. The water was right there, practically in our back door. A house just the right size nestled among huge oak trees about one hundred feet from the water. Most of the time we had just enough water in the cove to get our second-hand pontoon boat from the dock to deep water. It became a weekend haven and a perfect place for the longer writing assignments that eventually demanded my time and effort. No neighbors disturbed us in the fall and winter months.

Peace and tranquility permeated my spirit there. Not only was I able to destress from my busy lifestyle, but also I felt closer to God in this serene place surrounded by the beauties of nature and away from the distractions of fast living.

More remarkably, that beautiful lake country is also where Jim and I sometimes attended church outside the denomination in which we had grown up. It was where we learned that many people who didn't hold all the understandings of Scripture that we held loved the Lord and were good students of the Bible. It was where we found people who loved us and treated us with greater concern than we found in our home church. What an eye-opening experience!! God was enlarging our borders.

By this time, I had moved out of the high school classroom into an administrative position. Never before, in my wildest imagination, had I thought I would want to be involved in high school administration. Strangely enough, the timing was right, and the work was an unexpected and fulfilling challenge. Wonder of wonders! I loved it. For the first time since my first teaching job, I couldn't wait to go to work. And I continued to look for ways to expand my borders.

Did I dare to expand my dream? Why not? I decided to see if I could get admitted to the educational specialist degree program at Georgia State University. I reasoned that it was only with new degrees that I could increase my chances of advancement and higher salaries; the latter would lead to a substantial increase in our income and could contribute to a better retirement. Achieving that goal was not a piece of cake, but it could happen. I continued moving onward and upward.

Did I seek God's wisdom about this possibility? Sure, I prayed about it. Then I plunged headlong into plans and figured if it was not His will, God would find a way to stop it. That was my notion of how God works. I took comfort in the opinions of a great many of my Christian friends and acquaintances who held exactly the same view.

It took many years for me to learn the truth about that belief. Finally, I saw what had been in God's Word all the time. I was wrong. I should seek first His will for my life.

Just as we choose whom we will serve (Joshua 24:15), we choose to walk in faith on God's path or we take paths of our own choosing. God has revealed His will in Scripture. We are not really in the dark about His will unless we want to be. If we are sick and in need of healing, He wills for us to experience His healing, and many verses of the Bible support that assertion (See 1 Peter 2:24; Psalm 107:20; Psalm 103:2–3). If we are in financial woes, His will is for us to have what we need and enough to help others. If we are in the throes of sin, addiction, or despair, He has provided deliverance through Jesus Christ. Paul recognized His provision when he wrote, "And this same God who takes care of me will supply *all your needs* from his glorious riches, which have been given to us in Christ Jesus" (Philippians 4:19 NLT, emphasis added).

What more can we conceivably need Him to promise? He promises to supply *every need*. Even the psalmist even goes so far as to promise that God will give us the very desires of our hearts if we delight in Him (Psalm 37:4). Our delight in Him will cause our desires to align with His desires.

Of course, I'm not talking about things like what to eat for dinner or whether to get a haircut this week or stretch it to the next. I'm not even talking about what house someone should live in. I am, however, talking about His concerns for our everyday affairs and whether we honor Him with our lives or not. His Word teaches us to bring our concerns and cares to Him and let Him handle them: "Casting all your cares on Him for He cares for you" (1 Peter 5:7). The New Living Translation says it this way: "Give all your worries and cares to God, for he cares about you."

Continuing with the mentality of asking God to open the door if it was His will for me to work to earn higher degrees, I pursued admission to a specialist degree program in education. He opened the door, and I started the program. After completing a few classes, I heard from one or two classmates that the university offered a program that afforded the ability to earn the specialist degree while in the doctoral program. Just two weeks too late, I inquired whether I could change my program and work on two degrees at once. The university denied my request. The department had totally revamped their doctoral program, making it impossible to work on both degrees at the same time at GSU. Setback. Or so I reasoned. Deeply disappointed, I lumbered on to the EdS degree. More hours in the classroom. More research. More paper writing. More speaking. Done!

Stretching Toward Another Dream

During that accomplishment, another dream had sprouted. I finally believed I could do it all. With God's help and another two years of study, I could earn the coveted PhD. A frenzy of activity began: application, letters of recommendation, submission of transcripts, nail-biting while waiting. My "chatterbox" told me it would never happen, that I was too old, that I was too busy, that it would take too long, that I could never compete well with the younger and smarter people who earned doctorate degrees. I was constantly nagged with questions: Will I be accepted? Do I stand a chance? Can I actually pull it off even with God's intervention?

Praise God! Admission granted. Was that step God's will for my life? Was it His permissive will or his perfect will? I didn't stop to consider. I had asked Him to open doors or close them. If he closed certain doors, then I would accept that particular step was not in His will for my life.

The doors opened without one squeak. I set out to reach this goal in two years, all the while working at my job ten to twelve hour days for three or four days a week. Jim found supper somewhere. I didn't cook it for him on the days I had classes at the university or the days when I had athletic supervision at my school. Sometimes he drove the twenty miles to eat his evening meal with me and attend a game in which he didn't know any of the players or their parents. He did it just to be with his wife who had supervision duties but had to move about in the crowds and couldn't sit in one place any length of time. His life must have been lonely. Mine was stimulating. Most of the time I functioned on overload.

Meanwhile, our grown children and their wives hit a spiritual wall. They were trying on worldly wings. Right under my busy nose, they were leaving behind the godly principles and lifestyles we had tried to instill in them. I was not totally oblivious. I was just busy. I prayed for them and tried to trust God to bring them back home to Him. I stretched on to my educational goal.

Only one glitch hampered the timing of that goal. My advising professor did not show up for an important appointment. I had paperwork that required her signature of approval for me to graduate on my timeline. The deadline hour passed. Utterly frustrated, I sent up a quick prayer for favor. Then I appealed to the acting head of my department.

He refused to act in her behalf. I would not graduate that semester. Disappointed, utterly frustrated, and powerless, I stewed! Was it worth the angst? I questioned God. Was I lacking somewhere? Was there something in my life that hindered His answer to that prayer? He was silent. In my trying time, I had to allow patience to go to work (Romans 5:3; James 1:3). I was forced to walk by faith and not by sight.

A full semester stretched ahead of me. I added an elective course to the scores that I had already completed, secured all the recommendations, finished all the requirements, and earned my degree in January. That I had to wait until June for the degree to be officially conferred was a bitter pill to swallow. One whole year later than planned, the Lord, my husband, and I claimed the coveted degree. Never would I ever say I did it by myself. It was God who opened doors and gave me the stamina and intellectual ability to achieve those goals. It was my husband who supported me every step of the way. It was my family who supported me but quietly went their own way while I was busy and drifted from us and from God. By that time, I was already a grandmother and no longer middle-aged by some standards. My mind said, "So what if I'm older?" I would be an old lady one day anyway—with or without that desired degree. I still did not recognize the full degree of the drifting of our children.

And it was God who had given me the husband to beat all husbands. Through it all, he was right there urging me on. Encouraging me to realize *my* dreams. Soothing me and reassuring me when I felt overwhelmed. Reminding me that I could do everything with the help of Jesus, who is my strength. In hindsight, I often wonder what dreams he abandoned so that I could fulfill mine. He skirts the issue. He says I am number two in his life; God is number one. I'm fine with that confession. I often ask myself, what did I ever do to deserve such an utterly unselfish and encouraging man? He and I have both known for years that one of his strongest spiritual gifts is that of encourager. And, if there's a scholar in this family, it is he, not I.

But I digress.

Do you have a dream on the back burner? Are you intimidated? Do you fear you cannot possibly realize it? Or are you just not ready to commit? Do you believe the Scriptures?

God's Word promises that if we delight in the Lord, He will give us the desires of our hearts; if we commit our way to the Lord and trust Him, He will bring our dreams to pass (Psalm 37:4–5). I have learned over the course of many years that the key is delighting in Him. Committing ourselves to the path He has chosen for us no matter what the future holds also helps. It may be that, like so many Christians suffering and giving their lives for the cause of Christ today, we are called on to make the ultimate sacrifice. Our delight in Him and our confidence that He knows us and loves us will sustain us even in times of peril if we put our complete trust in Him. It is only when our will begins to line up with His that what He wants for us is what delights us and becomes what we desire with our whole heart.

Realizing dreams is not for the wimpy. Or the procrastinator. Perhaps the ability to succeed in education is the area of God's gifting to me. Was God driving me to complete the degrees? I really don't think so. I can remember a time when I thought of all the university professors I had sat under in my university "career," all those I eventually worked with. Many of them were atheists at worst and agnostics at best. A very few were committed Christians.

As I pictured those with whom I had connected, I believe God's Spirit nudged me, "Somebody has to reach them." At the time, it seemed to me that the best people to take to them the message of Christ would be those who were educated, those who could speak on their level. Maybe me? I really couldn't bear the thought. It frightened me. I was finding it hard to act on what I knew in my heart to be true, that I could do the all things with Christ giving me the strength and ability. Once again, I allowed my adversary to whisper in my ear. I reasoned that I would not know what to say if they wanted to debate my Christian faith. I didn't want to appear to be ill-equipped to handle their rebuttals and the questions I was sure they'd raise.

I wish I could say that I evangelized my dorm and the whole university while I was there as an undergraduate. I can't. While I didn't party with my classmates, I managed to share my faith with only a very few students. I did find a church to attend; I felt it was important not to get out of the "habit" of church attendance. I still do. I also became a member of Fellowship of Christian Students and participated in many outreach activities near the campus. As I look back on all my university days, even into graduate school, I think I was more or less what Craig Groeschel calls a "Christian atheist," meaning someone who has accepted Christ as Savior and expects to go to heaven one day but lives as if He does not matter in everyday life. I believed in God and continued to practice the Dos and Don'ts under which I had been reared, but

I had not yet become willing to follow the command of the Lord to "go into all the world and preach the gospel." I've heard and read stories of celebrated evangelists and pastors who began their ministries while they were students. I don't have that satisfaction today. My mind rebelled at the thought, but God did not give up on me. He will not give up on you.

I now firmly believe that God's commission to the disciples just before Christ disappeared from their sight and went back to sit on the right hand of God was delivered to all followers of Christ—even me. He told these men who had been His faithful companions for three years, "Go ye into all the world, and preach the gospel to every creature" (Mark 16:15).

Most of these disciples were not learned in the sense that we think of being educated today. They may have been businessmen or blue-collar workers. We know that four of them were fishermen; one was a despised tax collector. We know hardly anything about the others except for Simon the Zealot who was an insurrectionist, Judas who betrayed Jesus, and Thomas who doubted the resurrection. But we do know one thing. Jesus did not call them just to go to their own kind. He called them and commissioned them to go into "*all* the world and preach the gospel to *every* creature." Then he gave them the power and the authority to cast out devils, to resist and shake off sicknesses from snake bites and poison, to speak with new tongues, and to lay hands on the sick who would, subsequently, recover (Mark 16:17–18).

In His last words to His followers before ascending to heaven, Jesus told them to preach the good news to everyone. The "every creature" that He spoke of were not just fishermen. They were not just other tax collectors. They were not just carpenters or farmers. Some were Roman soldiers. Some were thieves. Some were murderers. Some were prostitutes. Some were kings. They were people from different social classes with differing degrees of moral uprightness.

That commission was to the diverse twelve who followed Christ; it is also to followers of Christ today. But many of us take a deep breath of relief when we read that Scripture. We argue that God has not called us to preach. Today, most of us have relegated the call to "preach" to the domain of a person who accepts a call from God to evangelize or proclaim the gospel to a congregation as its pastor. I think it helps (or does it hurt?) to learn that the Greek word translated "preach" means simply to make a public proclamation in an authoritative manner (Strong's Concordance). Our authority is the Word of God. Our power comes from the indwelling Spirit of God. We need nothing else besides a willing spirit and a desire to obey God's Word to "preach."

So, in the context of Scripture, "preach" simply means to share sincerely and publicly the good news of Christ's life, death, and resurrection and what He's done for us. We have around us groups of people in our neighborhood, in small groups of our church family and, possibly, all of our Facebook followers. Did Jesus say you had to stand behind a pulpit and tell the good news? No. Did he say you must videotape or record audio of a message to the world about Jesus to fulfill the command to preach? No. He did not. I may be taking liberties with the intent of the original language of the Scripture, but I believe "preach" also means to declare the gospel to one person at lunch or to a small group of friends who have gathered. We can proclaim God's goodness while we take a rest break from volleyball, basketball, touch football, or dominoes. We can share the good news of Christ and His grace to the person who delivers mail, to the cashier at the grocery store, or to the salesperson in the department store. To a complete stranger? Yes! To our closest family members? First and foremost.

Another way that we share the gospel is to live like Christ. We can practice asking ourselves, "What would Jesus do?" in every situation and decision we face and then do it. Better still, we can ask Him to *show* us what to do. Then we have the ability to make decisions and act upon them in the way His spirit leads. Sometimes, we don't have to say a word; our actions often speak much louder than any words we can utter. Sometimes, we speak our faith; always, our challenge then is to walk the talk, to align our actions with our words. We can do it with God's help; with His help, each one of us can do anything He purposes for us to do (Matthew 19:26; Mark 10:27). Each individual believer can and must rise to the challenge. God doesn't give anyone a bye.

Jesus didn't say to His disciples (and to us), "I would like you to go share my good news with the peoples of this world." He didn't say, "I hope you will love me enough to tell a lost and dying world that I want to save them." No. He clearly commanded: "*Go* into all the world." That might mean tell our immediate world: home, family, school, work place. That might mean tell those in our community's nursing homes, jails, playgrounds, ball fields, and charities. That might mean tell our government agencies, even get involved in political positions on the local, state, or national level. That could mean people in foreign countries. God will let you know where He wants you. Are you willing to *go*?

At this juncture, if you're feeling you'd like to answer God's call but don't know what to do or how, I have good news. God will tell us what to do, and He never calls us to do something that He won't equip us to do. His call is pretty clear. It is simple. *Go*! Your faith in Him and His love for you makes you ready. Then you decide. Will you determine to act on a belief that with His help you can do it? Is Paul's proclamation that he can do all things through Christ only for Paul? Will you say with him those same words and know that Christ strengthens you for the "all things" that He puts in your path? Will you accept that you have the authority and the power to proclaim life (Jesus said, I am the way, the truth and the life) to a dying world? A world that, without our love and compassion motivating us to share with them the good news, is going to spend eternity in hell?

I challenge you to declare, "I will answer the call to share the gospel with my world." Believe that God has empowered you already, as Jesus said. Believe that you can do it because God's Word says you can. When you believe it, you receive it. When you receive it into the soil of your life, you grow it. When you grow it, you do it. The blessings of obedience become yours. Others are blessed. God gets all the glory!

Chapter 13

STRETCHING THE MOTHER IN ME

Trust in the Lord with all your heart.
–Proverbs 3:5 ESV

———◆———

W hen a couple decides they want a baby, they may not even have a clear motive or an answer to why they want to disrupt their lives. Sometimes, they don't stop to think about having a baby; they just carelessly enjoy each other until—OOPS—one day a little one is on the way. Some of these parents are happy; others find themselves suddenly and totally derailed, disappointed, disillusioned, and stuck.

For Jim and me, a baby was out of the question when we first married. I was in college in West Virginia, and I had promised my dad that I would finish what I had started. Jim was still in the US Navy, stationed on an aircraft carrier based in Norfolk, Virginia. The carrier mostly spent long stretches—six or eight months at a time—in the Mediterranean or the waters around Cuba and Haiti. So we definitely did not want a child immediately.

Then, when we thought the timing was right to start trying, a doctor told me that I might never be able to conceive. My anatomy was slightly out of kilter. So, I mourned briefly, we prayed for a miracle, and we tried not to worry about it. We worked, enjoyed each other's company, and made friends with the slightly older young marrieds at our church.

In August, when I was preparing to go back to work at the end of the summer a year or so later, I experienced nausea that attacked me at different parts of the day. The intermittent sickness went on for nearly a week before I made an appointment to see a doctor. The older family doctor listened to my symptoms, asked a few questions, and declared I had a virus. He prescribed some anti-nausea drugs and told me that

I could expect to be over the virus in a few days. Imagine my surprise when intermittent nausea continued into another month or more before I went back to the doctor. The "virus" had blossomed into a baby. I had conceived after all, and we were about to receive the miracle that we had asked for. Unlike more modern parents, we would not learn that our bundle of joy was a boy until the day of his birth.

The timing could not have been worse for my career. At that time in the history of teaching and in the system in which I was working, pregnant women, even married pregnant women, were forced to take leave or quit teaching when their body changed enough that it was clear that they were not just gaining weight. We could not be in a classroom with impressionable young people if we were obviously pregnant. What a difference a few decades have made. Can you imagine the furor today if employers made such rules and regulations? Can you see the headlines? Social media would have a field day. So there I was, at the beginning of a school year wanting to finish the year and aware that I could hide my "condition" only until the Christmas break. I would not get my full year of experience; I worried that I would not be allowed to continue even until the end of the semester. Stifled by regulations, I made my plans to resign at the beginning of the break.

A cool spring in Cleveland, Ohio, arrived. At the appointed time, a robust baby boy, which neither of us knew a thing about caring for, entered our lives and totally disrupted our lifestyle. Confident that I knew how to care for a baby since I had helped so much with younger siblings at home, I soon saw my confidence crumble. This was a boy. All my siblings were girls. That was one challenge. Then we faced the rigors of caring for a baby with colic, and with no sound information on how to cure it or how to handle it, my determination to be a good mom evaporated with each crying episode.

Nothing short of a car ride would soothe him enough to get him to rest without hours (or so it seemed) of discomfort and squalling. For about three months, I found myself wanting to scream and yell with my crying baby; I was willing to do almost anything to get him to hush. I confess the thought only because I know that many parents resort to horrific practices when their babies are inconsolable, and they feel as if they're about to lose their minds. Thankfully, reason and the Spirit of God prevailed; this baby was tiny and robust but fragile. Still, I didn't know what to do to end his suffering.

Dr. Spock didn't tell me all I needed to know. I was over 350 miles from my mom and grandmother and any other family support. At my wits end, sometimes I cried with my precious baby. I also prayed for him that his pain would cease—for his sake as well as mine. In spite of having been a Christian most of my life, I did not think of asking God to give me the wisdom to deal with our littlest sweetheart. I'm ashamed to admit that. I just asked God to cause him to hush. Jim had not yet given his heart to the Lord, so he didn't pray. Somehow, the Lord saw us both through those challenging early days. Inspired and nudged, not only by the Holy Spirit but also by being a father and feeling the weight of doing fatherhood right, Jim surrendered to Christ quickly after Larry was born. We learned how to stretch into parenthood together with God on our side.

Two years and eleven months later, the second miracle baby came into our lives. Again, this one suffered colic. Again, we did not know what to do, but he seemed to find some relief when we lay down with him on our stomach and patted his back. Fortunately, his discomfort passed in two or three months, and we settled into a more comfortable routine. We found joy in our babies. We played music for them and read to them. We took them to church and encouraged them to pray at a very early age.

That encouragement paid off. When he was close to three years old, our baby, Lynn, experienced painful earaches. We tried different home remedies, including having someone who smoked to blow smoke in his ear; we put warm sweet oil in the ear. He experienced a few hours or a day or two of relief; then the ache would begin again. In the wee hours of one morning when Jim was out of town, Lynn could get no relief, so he and I walked, prayed, and praised. I held him in my arms with his head on my shoulder and prayed for him to get relief once and for all. This illness was not life threatening. It was just an earache, and I had survived earaches as a child.

Determined and inspired to believe God's promise for healing that night, I walked the floor—from the den to the living room to the dining room and back to the den. Around and around we went. I instructed him to say "Thank you, Jesus" every time his ear hurt. So as the pain ravaged his little ear, his sweet soft voice found some volume. He followed my lead.

"Thank you, Jesus. Thank you, Jesus."

I could tell when the pain was particularly strong because his voice would get stronger, and his tone would reflect his agony.

"Thank you, Jesus!"

I continued, "Thank you, Jesus for Lynn's healing. Thank you for making his ear well."

With bulldog tenacity we walked and praised. We cried and praised. For the longest time—I think it may have been two or three hours—we persisted. Completely exhausted, Lynn finally went to sleep in my arms as I walked. Never again, to my knowledge, did he ever suffer another earache.

As he grew, our baby boy became a child of faith. When he was a little more than three years old, I was on the sofa suffering with a headache. Coming to stand near me, he asked what was wrong. I told him I had a headache. Immediately, he asked, "Do you want me to pray for you?" I remember that so well because he surprised me. When I said I would love to have him pray for me, he laid his little hands on my forehead and prayed. Immediately, I felt the headache leave.

A year or so later, the little one surprised me again. One Sunday night when he was close to his fifth birthday our family was at church. I was serving in the nursery when one of the young women came to the door and told me my husband wanted me upstairs. She offered to take care of the children for the rest of the service. She wouldn't say why Jim wanted me in the sanctuary.

Just as I went through the door, Pastor announced that those who wanted to join the church should step to the front; he was about to administer the covenant of fellowship. I saw Lynn walking toward the pastor. Our younger child had already tugged at his dad's hand and asked if he could go up. Satisfying himself that our baby should not be stopped from such an important step, Jim had sent for me. I joined the service in time to hear my baby, along with several adults, promise to take the whole Bible rightly divided as their rule of faith and practice. Tears of joy spilled down my cheeks.

Many people questioned whether he was too young, whether he actually knew what he was doing. I also had the same questions, but I knew that child's prayers and his desire to please God. I had seen his faith, his tender heart, and his desire to help others even at his young age. Many years later, I learned that he had often given the money he needed to pay his own bills to people who were less fortunate than he was.

Our younger son was not the only one to experience a health victory. Another challenge to our faith confronted us; this time it was the older one. Now, I realize that our challenges were nothing like those of parents whose children are born with congenital defects or get a cancer diagnosis or lose a limb in a freak accident. Ours differed but still challenged our faith.

When Larry, the older of the two, was about five years old, his kindergarten teacher called me at work to say that Larry wasn't feeling good and that he had become more lethargic as the day passed. I picked him and his brother up early and took them home. After a brief time at home, I noticed that Larry's hands and joints seemed to be swollen; splotches of purplish color began to appear on his torso and limbs.

Early the next day, his feet swelled, and he couldn't walk without crying from pain. He also cried when I touched the splotchy parts of his body. I prayed for him and prepared to go to work the following day. That night he slept fitfully, and the next morning he was not better. I called for a substitute teacher and let my boss know I had a sick child. Going to the phone to call the boys' pediatrician, I heard a gentle voice inside me say, "Trust me." So I put the phone down and prayed for Larry. As the day waned, we didn't see any progress, so again I called my boss to say I wouldn't be in because of my child's illness. I would take the rest of the week off. Surely, I reasoned, he would be better in four days, and we both could return to school on Monday.

Jim continued to go to work. I stayed at home with both boys. As the symptoms worsened and Larry could not eat, I had to fight fear with all my might. My enemy reminded me that a member of our church, a young father just twenty-seven years old, had had similar symptoms a couple of months before Larry became ill. The young father had died. So I resolved again and again to call the doctor. Each time I picked up the phone to call, I heard a still, small voice saying, "Trust me." Then I considered that our first born might have an illness that I could not trust the Lord for. Could I trust God better if I did not have a name for the illness, if I did not know whether it was life threatening or not? I resolved to try.

The battle raged on into the third week. Each time I called to say I could not work, the principal's secretary wanted to know what was wrong with Larry. What did the doctor say? I could only say, "We have decided to trust God for his recovery." Every time I said that, I felt like a hypocrite because fear stalked my every step and intruded into almost every waking moment and into the long nights when sleep eluded me. I cried out to God asking Him to heal my baby. It seemed at the time that my prayers reached no further than the ceiling.

For years I had read Peter's words about Jesus "by whose stripes you *were* healed" (1 Peter 2:24; past tense verb, emphasis added). These words had not, though, become part of my belief system. We *were healed* already. Larry had been healed through the pain and suffering Jesus had endured in Pilate's judgment hall. But Larry might have a life threatening illness, and my religious training had taught me to ask Jesus for healing. As I monitored his symptoms, what I saw fed my fears and overwhelmed me, and this time kept me from confidently thanking God for that healing and moving forward in faith.

Seeking support, I talked with my loving mom, and she prayed. Then, after a few days, she began to warn me to get medical attention for Larry to protect myself and Jim from legal charges if he should die. I knew she meant well; she was looking out for me, but that was not what I wanted to hear. I longed for her to assure me that God would hear our prayers, that Larry would be well. Little did I know that she was battling a fear all her own.

About the middle of the third week, Larry seemed to labor to breathe. He was listless—almost lifeless. His body and face were so pale and thin—almost translucent. His inability to eat had taken what little flesh had covered his thin frame. So, Jim and I called for members of the church who we knew had trusted the Lord for their healing for years. We asked them to come to our house to pray even though it was about nine o'clock at night when we called. We also asked Jim's sister, a nurse, knowing that she had to go to work and coming to our house added miles to her drive.

These faithful friends and family gathered and prayed fervently. They reminded God (maybe they actually reminded themselves) of His promises to believers, promises that the work of healing had already been accomplished back in Pilate's judgment hall, that Peter declared that we had already been healed. During the prayer, I felt that God had heard us and that Larry was healed. My spirit was calmer and more assured.

Fear took a backseat for a time. The praying friends left, and our nurse sister left for work. I don't know about Jim, but I slept a bit easier that night and woke up the next morning expecting Larry to ask for food and to be able to move about a bit on his own. That did not happen.

I was able to coax him to eat some bites of soft food later and for the next few days, and, little by little, he got stronger until he could finally sit up without my help. However, his feet and joints were still swollen, and the purplish splotches remained on his body. He still cried out in pain when he tried to move on his own.

When I called for a substitute teacher on my sixteenth absence from work, the secretary, with compassion in her voice, reminded me that my contract provided that I would lose my teaching job if I didn't work at least one day out of every twenty. I didn't know how much longer I would need to be at home with Larry. But my son's health was far more important than my job. For the next three days, I walked the floor and prayed and did all I could to minister to my little boy's needs without neglecting the littlest one.

On the evening before the twentieth day and with all the passion, intensity and zeal I could muster, I prayed again for Larry's healing. I tried to maintain confidence in the Scripture that promises: "The effective, fervent prayer of a righteous man avails much" (James 5:16 NKJV). Then I called the babysitter and asked her if she could handle carrying him to the table and to the restroom and feeding him bland food like toast or applesauce or pudding since he still was unable to eat very much. She agreed to try it for one day. I would trust my precious firstborn to God. I would go back to work on the twentieth day since my first absence from my job.

That morning I prayed for both boys as I dressed them. I prayed for myself to have the wisdom to know how to answer well-meaning people who wanted to know what was wrong with my little one. With my enemy sitting on my shoulder and whispering in my ear, I drove to work in tears. When my youngest asked, "What's wrong, Momma?" I must have answered him, but today I have no clue what I said. I just remember his standing on the hump in the back of the car and patting my shoulder. Those were the days long before car seats for children were even a gleam in someone's imagination.

Somehow, I made it through the day—a Friday. I clung to the solitude of my classroom between classes and at lunch. I didn't want to be bombarded with questions. Unwilling to be like the double-minded man described in the Bible (James 1:8), I struggled during the day to keep my faith in God's provision for my son intact while fear constantly battled to win my mind.

That day was a turning point for me and for our son. The swelling in his feet began to dissipate, and he started walking a bit. The skirmishes continued: two more long weeks of praying, trusting, and acting on that trust by dropping him at the babysitter and doing battle with fear. Jim and I had put him into God's wheelbarrow; God was taking him across Niagara Falls. Slowly and almost imperceptibly, he recovered. We had to watch closely for the signs that he had turned the corner. With each small step forward, Jim and I praised God. We taught our baby who was not much more than two years old yet to thank God. At our encouragement, Larry also thanked and praised God for each milestone in his recovery. Finally, six weeks of daily battle became part of our family history.

Only three years later, Larry played football in the county youth league. Soon after, he played softball on a church team. Never did his pediatrician find any lingering effects of illness when he was required to have physical examinations to play sports. To this day, we don't know what ailed him. We just know that we battled for his life with prayer, God's Word, and all the faith we could muster from day to day. Our Larry has lived to become a man with his own children and two beautiful grandchildren. Our family experienced that the Lord is good and faithful, that His mercy endures forever. We experienced then and many other times that we can trust Him as He faithfully performs His Word (Jeremiah 1:12).

Many other times in Larry's life, he found himself in situations that required his mom and dad to put their faith to work in a great way. On one of those occasions, we were living in Maryland, and Jim was making concrete tables and benches in our basement workshop in his spare time. He had a round table top leaning on a bench to finish curing and had just warned the boys to be careful when the table top fell against one of Larry's legs. Immediately, the leg began to be blue and purple, and Larry could not stand on it. On close examination, it appeared to us his leg might be broken. It looked different from the other one. Immediately, we went to prayer and claimed the healing that we saw promised in Scripture.

After we prayed, Jim and I stood on each side of Larry to support his weight. We encouraged him to thank God as he tried repeatedly to put weight on the affected leg. His brother cried with him; we cried with him, but we were determined to win the battle for supernatural healing. We determined to hold fast to our confession of faith. So he hobbled about as we all praised God for his healing. I don't have any idea how long we walked and prayed and praised, but after a long time, he began to put more weight on the "broken" leg. Before that evening passed, Larry's crooked leg seemed to have straightened. The shin no longer sported deep blue and purple coloring; it was no longer swollen; it no longer hurt him to put his weight on it. Before he went to bed, our first-born was as good as new. We rejoiced as we were all reminded again of God's faithfulness.

Living out of this stretch was, at that time, not much more difficult than the telling of it. Should we have gone to the emergency room with our son? That would have been the reasonable thing to do. We then had and still have nothing against physicians and medical intervention when it is necessary, but we had learned about supernatural healing. At a different time in our lives, we probably would have made a different choice. At this particular time, we were trying our best to live by faith. We had moved to Maryland at God's specific direction. We had experienced the faithfulness of God and answered prayer about where to live, what church to become a part of, what jobs to take. We had learned we could trust God to supply our needs; He had proven that to us again and again. So, to us, looking to God for Larry's healing was a no-brainer. As I look back on that time, I remember that it simply was the thing to do. We didn't even question our decision. We just did it.

Have we had perfect lives? Has our faith been perfect all the years of our marriage? No, to both questions. We've had our share of faith challenges and years of "proving God." And we've discovered that few places offer more fertile fields for challenge and stretch than family life. Family presents many opportunities for celebration. Thank God for those times. Conversely, it offers challenges, challenges that cause disruption and heartbreak, challenges that threaten to tear apart your world like a T-5 tornado. Jim and I have had to dig ourselves out from the rubble and threats to our faith time and again.

Seeing your children through accidents and illnesses is nothing compared with watching them turn their backs on Godly living and embracing the ways of the unsaved world. When you've been very candid in your discussions with your children about ungodly choices, about the dangers of drinking and driving, dabbling in drugs, sexual promiscuity; when you do everything you know to do to "train them up in the way they should go" so they won't depart from biblical precepts when they're older, what do you do? Jim and I decided that God's Word is true. We determined in our hearts not to be discouraged by the raging of the storms in our lives and the lives of our children. Today, I declare you can trust God's Word. When you don't seem to have faith in your own prayers, that's the time to put your faith in God's faithfulness. We have had to renew that faith many times in the last few years. Without our permission, circumstance has stretched our faith again and again.

Like their parents, both children experienced challenges to their faith and times of spiritual dryness. Both made choices to dabble in the pleasures of sin for a season and embrace a lifestyle that was anything but godly. Like many others, they had their faith tested and had to decide whether to believe in the God of the Bible or to believe the gods of this world. Perhaps their biggest challenge was feeding their faith on the Word of God and becoming completely surrendered to God. As I reflect on our lives together, I know that my faithful adherence to the "letter of the law" hindered my effective parenting. Because I had not yet really learned to feel secure in God's love and because I feared God's judgment, I was unable to help our boys know how to form an appropriate relationship with the Lord when they were younger.

Chapter 14

TESTING A
FAMILY'S FAITH

In the Lord put I my trust.
–Psalm 11:1

———◆———

Family life is often the center of a person's worst nightmare. It has been for us, not once but many times. The first great test for me began in the early 1980s when Dad experienced a heart attack and was hospitalized. All of his family had prayed fervent prayers for him to "get saved again" for years. That night he told Mom that he wasn't ready to meet the Lord, and his confession opened the door for her to encourage him to make his way back to the Father's house. He agreed, and he and Mom prayed together in his hospital room. All of my family rejoiced to know that Mom's forty-year prayer was answered.

For the next few years, Dad devoted himself to becoming the best Christian and church member that he could be. In the middle of his growing faith, he had a colorectal exam that showed polyps, which the doctor removed. A lab test revealed that at least one polyp was cancerous. Cancer! A word that tends to strike fear in the hearts of people all over the world. It got our attention. The whole family, including the church family and other churches of relatives in distant cities began to pray for him as he was treated. When he went back later for a follow-up exam, the doctor could find no evidence of cancer—not even a scar where the polyps had been removed. Our family celebrated his healing.

Then came the days in early 1989 when he experienced illness that the doctors had trouble identifying. Dad was often horrifically sick to his stomach, mostly after meals. As if he had some premonition, he began to tell family members he would not be around much longer. Finally, his local doctors sent him to a university hospital where a team of oncologists found cancer in his colon. Cancer had returned. This finding, they said, was indisputable. He continued to be ill and seemed to get no relief. Again, his family, his church, and his friends bombarded heaven for his healing and encouraged him to exercise faith in God. Several months later, he was in the hospital fighting for his life.

For six long weeks or more, our dad stayed in the hospital with its loving and caring staff of doctors and nurses. My oldest sister and I took turns staying the nights in his room and attending to every need—those we could possibly handle, including many that no father should ever have to experience at the hands of his daughters. We served him out of love and compassion, never once giving a thought to how difficult it might have been for him to receive our services. We simply wanted to make him comfortable and do it quickly because the nursing staff was so obviously overworked. (May God forgive us for the assaults on his dignity.) All the while, we prayed for his healing. All of our family and church friends encouraged Dad to believe that the same God who had healed him once would heal him again. We did not remember that Jesus Himself had said that believers would have the power to heal, that He promised we would "lay hands on the sick, and they **shall** recover" (Mark 16:18). We had read the Scripture many times, but it was not yet real to us.

By early October of 1989, it was clear that we had not made much headway in our prayers for Dad's healing. My sisters and I had planned a big fiftieth anniversary party for Mom and Dad, but Dad was in the hospital. It seemed he was struggling to live, to "hang on" until after the anniversary for Mom's sake. We went on with the plans. Friends and family were invited. Food was prepared. A few days before the anniversary, family and friends were set on ready for the celebration. The doctors said they would release Dad for a few hours if they found him able to attend the party. We prayed that he would be able.

The big day arrived, and Dad was not able. But the nursing staff had covered that possibility. They decorated a large sitting room and reserved it for Mom and Dad and their immediate family. They also provided a beautifully decorated cake and punch in festive cups. At the appointed time, they wheeled Dad's bed down the hall to the "party room" where they and his doctors joined the festivity. It was a very short party, but it showed the love and kindness of the wonderful people who served my dad. Late that day, the invitees showed up at the venue, Mom came, and family and friends held a celebration honoring Mom and Dad's long years together. It was memorable for all the wrong reasons. Our hearts were in the hospital room with the absent guest of honor.

My oldest sister and I were privileged to help the nurse change Dad's bed a few days later. He had been on heavy pain medication for several days and had nearly stopped communicating with anyone. He did complain that the balloon on the wall with paper legs was out to get him. Soon after, I was singing "Amazing Grace" (one of his favorite hymns) to him and heard him mumble something about turning off that horrible sound. That day, he roused enough to say, "Mom, look at that beautiful river. Oh, it's so beautiful."

Mom had just gone home that night when we discovered that his bed needed to be changed. As we helped nurses finish the task and laid him on his back again, it seemed that his breathing had become shallower than ever. Then, in a minute or two, something like a sigh escaped his lips. His eyes rolled a bit. I asked the nurse, "Is that it? Has he gone?"

After what seemed an eternity, the nurse nodded. I went to the bed and begged Dad not to go like this, defeated by his enemy. All through his illness, I just knew that he would be healed. I knew that God heard my prayers for him. I had believed with all my heart that he would get up from that sickbed a victorious man. As he lay there, maybe between this world and the next, I asked him to receive his healing and then, a healed man, he could just lie down and go to sleep and be with the Lord. The minute I said that, I remembered a conversation we had had a few days before. I was talking to him and reminding him of God's healing power when he said, "Sis, I don't want to start over again." When I asked him what he meant by that, he protested, "You know what I mean." Well, I did not know, and I puzzled over that statement many times over the next few days.

That night, when I spoke to him, it seemed that he struggled to breathe again and to open his eyes. At that moment, I remembered his words. Suddenly, his statement gained meaning for me. I believed then and still believe he meant that he did not want to be healed or to think that he was healed and have to endure again possible agony such as that he had already experienced in the last few months of his life.

Sorry for my insistence and feeling a bit selfish, I touched his arm and assured him, "Dad, it's okay. Go on and be with the Lord if you want to. We understand." When I said those words, it seemed that I could feel his spirit soar out of the room. The release of his spirit from his house of clay was peaceful and victorious. Dad's illness and his battle with cancer were heartbreaking; his home going was not. I am forever grateful that Rita and I were with him when he left.

At that time, I was thankful that Dad was no longer suffering. I still am. Do I believe God answered our prayers for his healing with a resounding "NO!" Absolutely not. I believe the promise of Jesus, "and *all* things, whatsoever ye shall ask in prayer, *believing*, ye *shall receive*" (Matthew 21:22; emphasis added). The key to answered prayer is belief. Belief in the promises of God involves complete reliance on and trust in God's Word. When what we ask for does not happen, it is not God's fault. Often, someone else's will and desires collide with ours. He is faithful to His Word. We continue to trust Him!

That trust was to be tested again in 2009. It started with a frantic telephone call.

"Aunt Judy, don't panic. Uncle Jim's had an accident. We're all with him and are praying for him. He's in a lot of pain, but he's able to talk."

Those words sent my head and my heart into a spin. Immediately, I breathed a prayer for Jim and listened to the details. By the time I received the call, the group on the ATV trail had already called 911. Meanwhile, some of the family members did what they could to make Jim comfortable. Many of them were people of faith who knew to pray, so they prayed while they waited. The Emergency Medical Services team was able to reach him with the ambulance, but they were concerned that the rough ride out of the woods would add to the damage than his ATV had already done and make his pain even more unbearable. They were busy trying to stabilize him, so I told my nephew to tell Jim, "Not today. You are *not* going home to heaven today." My spirit was at peace; I fully believed that death would not claim my husband of more than forty years that day.

Many of my family members and a few friends had driven from Georgia, North Carolina, and Maryland to Southern West Virginia for a weekend reunion. They were intent on enjoying the private trail they had conquered only two years before. Jim had looked forward to the trip as much as the younger members of the group who were riding trail with him that day. I had elected not to go.

As it happened, the group had split mud holes wide open, mastered ruts and sharp turns, and thoroughly enjoyed the first two hours of the trip. At the time of the accident, they were deep in the mountains and far from state or county roads. They had come to a different side of the same mountain they had climbed two years before. Even though two or three riders on more powerful machines made it up the steep grade safely, Jim did not take time to assess the terrain. Rather, he accelerated his ATV and began to conquer the mountain. Unfortunately, near the ridge, the ATV sputtered, flipped, bounced twice on Jim, and rolled back down the way they had come.

Thankfully, someone in the crowd had enough phone signal to call 911 for help. Because those who showed up first assessed Jim's condition as too serious to ride what was little more than a trail out of the woods, they called for air transport and waited impatiently. Jim's battered body was probably more than eighty miles as a crow flies from the nearest trauma center. Immediately upon learning where EMS was transporting him, my baby sister and her husband drove me at breakneck speeds on the hard surfaces. We purposed to be at the hospital by the time Jim arrived there. Sure enough, in about an hour we saw the hospital with a helicopter hovering over the pad on the roof. We learned in a few minutes that it had delivered Jim.

An eternity later (actually it was a couple of hours), the emergency room notified us that he was severely wounded and yet alert and talking. For ten days, his body struggled in intensive care to recuperate from bruised heart, lungs, and kidneys. He had a broken clavicle and a total of sixteen other fractures including two vertebrae and several ribs. Given a morphine pump to deal with the overwhelming pain, my stalwart husband had to be coaxed several times to press the button when he needed it even after staff assured that it was impossible for him to overdose.

My mother and three of my sisters and their families lived about sixty miles from the hospital. In my mind that was too far for me to commute. Besides, I could not bear to leave Jim's side except for those three or four hours during the day when the intensive care unit would not allow anyone but patients in there. Fortunately, the hospital provided a shuttle to a nearby hotel, so I rented a room just to have a space to shower and rest for the hours I was banished from Jim's side. Caring family traveled the distance to bring me clothing and supplies and just to sit with us as often as they could. But it was lonely there.

Two local pastors whom we had never met brought encouragement with reminders from the Word of God and prayer. One of them pastored a distant member of the family. He visited more than once, and each visit was powerful. We could feel his love for people, and we could feel the presence of God with him. It was comforting to know that he also believed in God's power to restore and heal completely.

As I sat by his bed and read Scriptures to Jim and prayed for him, not once did I doubt that Jim Duncan would walk out of that hospital. I read the Bible to him whether he was asleep or awake. Most of the time he was so heavily sedated for the pain that I did not know whether he actually heard any of it. I reasoned that his spirit would hear. I prayed for him and for the others whose rooms were in a circle with his. Their doors and windows opened to the center so that I could see many of them from Jim's room. After eleven days in ICU, Jim went to a step-down unit for two days. For a couple of days, he had begged to go home, so it became my responsibility to tell the doctors and nurses to get his paperwork ready. I made flight reservations and gave the hospital the time we needed to be discharged so we could make the flight. At literally the last minute they signed Jim's release. With a back brace and in great pain, he endured the taxi ride to the airport and did his best to fold his complaining body into a seat by the window. The aisle seat allowed for more jostling and bumping than he could withstand.

At home in Georgia at last, my loving husband fought the good fight of faith. With family and friends praying with us and for us, we began Jim's long road to recuperation together. What doctors said he would not be able to do, he has done. God has blessed him to be fully recovered from the injuries sustained and one problem discovered as a result of the accident. We both put our faith in the Word of God and His promises: "He sent his word and healed them" (Psalm 107:20); "But I will restore you to health and heal your wounds, declares the Lord" (Jeremiah 30:17). We took comfort in another word from the psalmist:

> Bless the Lord, O my soul: and all that us within me,
> bless his holy name . . . and forget not all his benefits:
> Who forgiveth all thine iniquities; who healeth all thy
> diseases; Who redeemeth thy life from destruction; who
> crowneth thee with lovingkindness and tender mercies
> (Psalm 103:1-4).

Do I believe that God engineered the accident and put Jim in pain to teach us patience or some other lesson? That the accident was God's will for that particular time in our lives? No! Not then! Not now! I'm also convinced that the devil did not cause the accident. So often we blame Satan for something that is just not his fault. Jim agrees it was simply a mistake on his part not to acquaint himself with the terrain before beginning the climb. God used that mistake and its consequences to bring about good. Through it all, we and our family were reminded that God is faithful to His promises, that He never leaves or forsakes us, that we can, with His help, bounce back from near-tragic circumstances. Today, doctors marvel that Jim is in as good shape as he is, that he weathered that assault on his body and suffers nothing more than a back that tires easily and causes pain after unaccustomed activity. To God be all glory!

As I reflect on Dad's battle with cancer and Jim's accident many years later, I believe the way we pray may need to be overhauled. With faith in God and the Holy Spirit to empower us, we could have simply laid our hands on Dad and told the cancer to leave his body. We could have laid hands on Jim and claimed the promises of the Scripture for his body. Since Dad's death and Jim's accident, we have learned that our prayers do not move God to action; neither does our faith. God has already been moved to action. When Jesus hung on the cross, He said, "It is finished" (John 19:30). With his death and resurrection, Jesus paid the sin debt for all people. Receiving the thirty-nine wounds in His body before the crucifixion and giving up His life on the cross finished the work required for our salvation (our spiritual rebirth) as well as our deliverance from sickness, disease, accident, poverty, mental and emotional turmoil, and anything else that threatens our ability to fulfill His purpose for our lives. His work was finished. Everything that God has for us is ours when we *believe and receive by faith* the provisions and promises He has already made.

What we had not grasped at that time was the promise of Jesus to His disciples after His resurrection and just before His ascension back to Heaven. He said *believers* would lay hands on the sick and they *would* recover (Mark 16:18). He did not say it was necessary to agonize with God, to plead with Him and to beg for healing. With faith in God's Word and the Holy Spirit to empower us, we can simply lay hands on the sick. Our Savior has already accomplished the work of healing. Jesus promised they will recover, and all the promises of God are YES and AMEN in Christ (2 Corinthians 1:20). Yes. Yes. Yes, in Christ. It's clinging to our traditions—the way we've always done things, the things we've misunderstood or misinterpreted and cling to anyway— that make the Word of God of no effect in our lives (Mark 7:13).

Chapter 15

REFUSING SATAN'S BAIT

The Lord is the strength of my life;
Of whom shall I be afraid?
–Psalm 27:1

———◆———

Many Christian parents today are just like Jim and me. They rear their children the best way they know. They take them to church, read the Bible with them, pray with them, and encourage them to choose the ways of the Lord. Then, one day, those obedient children decide to stretch their wings. In their quest to become independent, they rebel—a little or a lot. Ours were not much different.

We always taught our children that it was fine to question our decisions as long as they showed the proper respect both in their word choices and in their tone of voice. Many times as the years passed we wondered if we had gone the correct route, and our answer to "Why?" so often became "Because I said so."

Like the children of our friends, our boys made choices that disappointed us. They sampled cigarettes and alcohol; they tried pot. For all we know, they chose to dabble with sex. Some would protest that, if they did those things, they were only "boys being boys." I tried to pass their behaviors off as growing pains; I just could not. As they boarded a spiritual seesaw, I feared that their souls were in jeopardy of hell. My spiritual training said they had backslidden and needed to be saved again. Jim and I watched as they lost interest in the church and their commitment to the Lord. We rejoiced when they renewed their commitment and did what we had been taught was right. Disappointments and temptations derailed them. They got back on track. They married and produced our beautiful grandchildren. Then both experienced the heartbreak of divorce. And they seemingly turned their backs on God. First one and then the other. We trained them in the way we believed they should go. They seemed to have departed from it.

Our older son experienced the heartbreak of divorce when his first son was just four years old. Devastated, he began to seek solace anywhere besides at church. Not among Christians who could have encouraged him and may have helped him to cope. This young man who had, at the age of thirteen, preached a sermon to a few thousand in a tristate convention center, began to look outside the Bible and God's people for ways to heal and philosophies to believe. After a few years, he took what seemed to be a leap of faith and married a second time. But his fervor for the Lord and being involved in ministry had disappeared. Only one thing has kept me hopeful that our training had not been in vain. Over the years his compassion for others has revealed his tender heart for those in need. Many times he has shared his home and helped to take care of people who could not, at the time, take care of themselves. He continues to go to church. He calls for prayer for himself and his friends. He is no longer leaving God out of his life.

While our younger son had bought a home and moved out of our house soon after Larry married, he continued in church and in leadership activities as director of the youth program at church. Soon, he married a beautiful girl whom he jokingly claimed to have evangelized. She had learned to love the Lord, and the two of them worked their day jobs and worked together in ministry at our local church. We were so thankful. Then, after our first granddaughter was born, their spiritual lives seemed to derail. Jim and I sought God separately and together for the assurance that our children would not depart from "the way they should go." It appeared that they had.

With our religion informing our beliefs, Jim and I had no choice but to think that both boys had lost their salvation, that their choices made them candidates for hell and not for heaven. I prayed for them constantly, and my prayers seemed to be in vain. Again and again, I reached for the promise that we could ask and we would receive (Matthew 21:22). The condition placed on that promise was faith. I determined that I would receive the answer to my prayer. I tried to exercise faith through years of spiritual ups and downs. Some were good years filled with peace; some were tumultuous and stormy. Then came the tsunami.

Hanging to God's Promises—By a Thread

It was the Saturday after a very quiet Thanksgiving Day, a day that would change our family life irrevocably. Our younger son, whom we always thought of as Lynn, even after he began to call himself Zach, and his son had planned to have Thanksgiving dinner with Jim and me. We had all been invited to dinner in Vidalia with Larry and his new wife's family, but I just had no desire to go. I remember feeling heavy in spirit and unhappy that our family life had been disrupted. Something in the atmosphere of our family was very wrong, and I was hoping to talk on Thanksgiving Day with Lynn about some of the choices he had made. That conversation was not to happen.

The background to that day formed over several long tumultuous months, a little more than a year if my memory serves me. Success in business and continuous socialization with wealthier counterparts in land development and construction seemed to have seduced Lynn into a lust for the things of the world that just could not be satisfied. The greater his financial success, the greater his accumulation of stuff and his association with powerful people, the further from God and the less happy he seemed to be. While Jim and I were proud of his hard work and his successes, we became concerned about the direction his life had begun to take. Our concerns were not unfounded. Eventually, he became unfaithful to his Lord and to his wife. I had been able to talk with him about almost anything over the years, but this time he closed me out entirely.

Lynn and his dad had business interests together for several years. We lived fairly close to each other for the first years of his marriage, divorce, and reunion with his wife. However, there came a time when we moved to a lake home about an hour from him and his family. We saw him and his family only on summer weekends at the lake house with crowds of people around and no chances for meaningful conversation. Our loving, gregarious son became a different person—still loving and polite but so close-mouthed, quiet and moody—definitely not the open, fun-loving young man he had been most of his life. I sensed that his spiritual life was suffering, so his dad and I encouraged him and his wife to choose a church near their home and make it a point to go regularly for their sakes and for their children's spiritual development. They said they would. I'm not sure that they did.

By the time this particular Thanksgiving Day had arrived, Lynn and his wife had separated for the second time; he had moved a girlfriend into his house, and his children had lost the security of a loving mom and dad living together in harmony. They had no choice in the disruption of their lives. By mutual agreement, Lynn took custody of our grandson; his wife took our granddaughter. Our grandchildren had their lives torn apart. (That's just what separation and divorce does to children — even when their parents have been unhappy and volatile together for a time.) They were devastated; their mother was devastated. Their dad was living a life of sin, and I struggled in my prayer life to know how to trust God for a different outcome. Somehow, I had forgotten to stand on God's promises, to walk by faith and not by sight. Like Job, I lived in fear of what might happen to my children (Job 1:5). I settled on praying for him daily and sending him cards and notes to encourage and assure him that God still loved him and his father and I loved him.

On the morning of Thanksgiving Day, Lynn called to say he and his son would be going to Vidalia after all, but they would come to our house the next day to visit for a few minutes. I don't know about Jim, but that day was very bleak for me. Without knowing why, I felt uneasy in my spirit all day. I walked the floor and prayed for the safety of my family and for restoration. I also indulged in a small pity party for myself and Jim because we had been "forced" to have Thanksgiving alone for the first time ever in our lives as a family. Throughout the day, I kept feeling as if a cloud of doom hung over us. I was finding it difficult to be thankful for anything that day.

Eventually, Thanksgiving passed, and Friday came. In the afternoon, Lynn and our second grandson came to our house briefly, not to visit but to borrow thermal underwear for hunting. They were in a hurry. I searched for and found the underwear, and the two left almost immediately. Lynn didn't offer me a hug. He didn't say, "I love you." He and our grandson just sped away in what I thought was his newly-acquired sports car. I was crushed. That day, it was all about me. I was shattered that he had decided to drive his son more than 300 miles round trip to spend Thanksgiving Day with people he hardly knew, people other than his mom and dad. My heart was broken that he had not even said more than two or three words to me. I had no idea he was sick. After he left, he called: "Mom, I'm sorry I left without saying goodbye."

Engrossed in self-pity, I retorted, "No, you're not!" He disconnected immediately without another word.

Those were the last words I ever spoke to my son. I said them in self-pity and anger and hurt. I never considered that he may have been hurting, that he had problems, that he may have been sick and scared. I can't begin to express how much I have wished to have an opportunity to change what happened in those moments.

In the early hours of the next morning, our baby son, now an adult with children of his own, breathed his last breath—away from home. Away from the people who loved him most. Away from the mother who regrets bitterly all these years later that she allowed self to get in the way of assuring her younger child of her love for him. The regret still pierces my soul. To maintain peace, I constantly have to cover that regret with God's Word.

On that Saturday, Jim and I learned of Lynn's death through a phone call from the young man who rented his basement. When I heard him say, "Gran, are you sitting down?" I knew something had to be horrifically wrong.

"No!" my spirit interrupted. "Please, no." His next words confirmed the nightmare. Our son had died during the night at the age of thirty-eight. The caller told me we would need to go to a police station in a small town about twenty miles from us to learn the details of Lynn's death.

It's still hard to write these words many years later. That day, I could hardly breathe; I couldn't pray. That dreadful trip to the police station is almost a blur today. But I remember well that I kept repeating words from Psalm 27 that I had learned in a song at Grace Fellowship Church a few months earlier. "Lord, You are the strength of my life. You are the strength of my life. You are the strength of my life." I said those words over and over. Convinced I would not be able to stop if I ever started, I dared not cry. I yearned for the assurance that the news of Lynn's death was a dreadful mistake. Remembering the testimony of Andrew Womack, a renowned television minister, about raising his own son from the dead five hours after he died, I determined to go to my own son and tell him to get up in the name of Jesus. The officer in charge absolutely refused to allow us into the morgue to identify him. The authorities were already satisfied that the body they had was that of our son.

My heart experienced a tug of war. As much as I wanted to, I did not persist. After all, I reasoned, my faith might be too weak to achieve the desired result. Our beloved younger son had died in his sleep in the wee hours of the morning at the home of a friend. An autopsy that took almost six weeks revealed that he had mixed prescription drugs with alcohol and cocaine. He may have even suffered with sleep apnea. At this point in my life, Lynn's death has been my worst nightmare.

Not only is our son lost to us forever; he went into eternity without the assurance that I loved him with my whole heart. Even today, the thought of his death is a poignant reminder to me that life is fleeting, that we need to assure frequently those we love dearly of our feelings for them. By the same token, we should resolve disagreements quickly and never go to bed angry with someone—anyone—but most especially those we love (Ephesians 4:26).

On the basis of my experience, I say to parents everywhere: You may feel that your children are driving you insane. They may seem to have deserted every principle you have ever taught them, but don't let your pride and anger and disappointment get in the way. Love them and reassure them of your love while you continue to pray for them, practice tough love when needed, trust them to God's care and exercise your faith in a faithful God.

To this day, I battle for peace over Lynn's death. For months, I had prayed constantly for him to leave his ungodly lifestyle and come back to the Lord. Often, I'd awaken in the middle of the night and plead with God to save him again. That's how my spiritual training taught me I should pray. I knew that he had once loved God. I knew that he had great faith as a child and young man. But all indications pointed to his "backsliding." The cause of his death seemed to settle the matter. For months after his death, I imagined him in hell. I imagined him suffering the tortures of utter darkness, utter aloneness, unending fires, and eternal separation from God. I didn't see how he could possibly escape eternal punishment. The very thought was unbearable. Both Jim and I endured agonies of grief, but Jim refused to believe that Lynn was in hell. We were so wrapped up in our own grief that we didn't have a clue what his brother was feeling. We left Larry pretty much to grieve on his own, which is another regret for me.

Over the next weeks and months, different people tried to console us. Some said they had asked God to give them a sign that their dead loved one had gone to heaven. I was afraid to know, so I didn't ask. But I wanted to. The one time I went to prayer to ask God for a sign, I seemed to hear a gentle voice reminding me, "We walk by faith, not by sight" (2 Corinthians 5:7). At that time, I couldn't figure out what that was supposed to mean to me and my loss, but I never asked for a sign. Then, after many months, I remembered Scriptures I had marked in my Bible over the years, Scriptures that held promise for my children and grandchildren (Isaiah 49:25 and 54:13 are two of them). Those words were for the Israelites, the Jews, but I took consolation in them. After all, my trust in Christ and my position as a child of God made me eligible for the promises of God to Abraham's descendants through Jesus Christ, the seed of Abraham.

In retrospect, God did provide a measure of solace for us from unexpected sources. The evening of the viewing our pastor, Gary Lewis, encouraged us with part of Psalm 42:7. He explained that "deep calls out to deep" and left us with the assurance that the Spirit of God calls out to the spirit of man and bypasses everything that would impede that communication. His words didn't mean much then, but they did weeks and months later. At the memorial service, Pastor Tommy Panter, our friend and mentor in foreign missions, encouraged Jim and me not to throw away our confidence in God (Hebrews 10:35). Jim found inspiration as he meditated on those words. I did not—even though I pondered them often. We both tried hard to maintain our faith in the God who had proved faithful in our lives and those of our loved ones.

God kept using various people and means to bring hope and help for our grief. Not quite a month after our Lynn's death, a young woman whom I had known for years followed Jim and me outside as we were leaving a friend's Christmas open house. She had helped provide music for the funeral. She told us that during the service for him, God had shown her a vision of Lynn floating toward heaven with his arms outstretched. I can't tell you how much I wanted to find comfort in her words, but I just could not. A year or two later, during a gospel music performance that I was watching, one of the musicians gave a testimony saying that had it not been for his mother's prayers, his lifestyle of drugs, drunkenness and prostitutes would have surely killed him and sent him to hell. He was thanking God publicly for his mother's prayers. As I listened to his testimony, a dam burst inside me. As I sobbed, I cried out to God, "Why not me, God? Why didn't You answer my prayers?"

Almost immediately, I heard a still small voice in my spirit: "What makes you think I didn't?" Startled, I stopped crying. "What makes you think I didn't?" rang in my mind over and over. With those words, a small glimmer of hope lit up my heart. I grabbed that glimmer and tried to nurture it. My spirit dared to hope but only briefly; my struggle continued. How could I reconcile what I believe the Spirit of God had said to me with what I had been taught all my life?

Sometime after that incident, I dreamed I saw someone going up in the sky toward heaven. I heard my mother's voice saying, "There goes Lynn." I looked up thinking she was talking about Dad, whose name was also Lynn. Then I heard myself saying, "That's not my dad. That's my son." I awakened feeling a sense of relief and hopefulness. After months of pain and suffering, I began to receive that dream and the other incidents as comfort from my heavenly Father. I dared to hope that my son had, somehow, made everything right with God before his death. I determined to hold on to God's promises. Over the years, I had experienced His faithfulness; maybe I could trust Him again. I was trying to walk by faith and not by sight, but I was not finding it easy to do.

In the ensuing months, I received an invitation to speak at a women's conference in West Virginia. I had just read *The Bait of Satan* by John Bevere. As I sought the Lord about what to say to the group, I felt the Spirit of God nudging me to talk about offense, a tactic that, as Bevere points out, Satan uses to trap us. I reasoned that if our enemy can cause us to nurse a grudge, he will find ways to grow that grudge into resentment and, finally, into offense. That offense could then become a root of bitterness. The writer of Hebrews warns that we must be careful not to allow a root of bitterness to grow up and corrupt us and cause others to be corrupted or harmed (Hebrews 12:15).

I knew that the nursed grudge and resentment and offense will eventually destroy a marriage, a family, a career, a church, a nation. Bitterness grows; its roots eventually destroy even the one who has become bitter. The Spirit of God reminded me that most people have many occasions in life, circumstances which are beyond their control, to allow grudges and resentment and offense to become part of their thinking. Their thoughts, over the course of time, plant the seed that, when nourished by anger and resentment, become full-blown bitterness. So, I prepared to speak about Satan's bait and its consequences in spite of my sadness and heartache.

By this time, I had been talking with friends and family members about the book and sharing Bevere's thoughts with them. In the course of our conversations, someone asked me if I had ever been offended. Thinking only of the modern usage of the word, I had to say, "Of course. Many times in my life." Then I began to wonder if I had fallen prey to Satan's bait. Could it be that my son's death had put me into a place where what I was feeling toward God was offense?

For days I examined my feelings and the Scriptures for further understanding. Finally, I realized that "offense" as used in Scripture has a different meaning from the common uses of the word today. In contemporary usage, offense means many things including the state of being insulted or morally offended; the act of displeasing or affronting (Merriam-Webster.com). As used in Scripture, it has a far more serious definition in its application to our relationship with God and our ability to maintain obedience to God's commands. In Scripture, offense, from the Greek *skandalon* means "that at which one stumbles or takes offense" (biblestudytools.com/dictionary/offence/).

Jesus said, "*I am the way*, the truth, and the life" (John 14:6, emphasis added). Yet, to many Jews He was a cause for stumbling and offense. They stumbled because they knew Him as the son of Joseph and Mary, not as the Son of God. They stumbled because He did not fulfill their mental expectations of the demeanor, status, and objectives of the King of the Jews. Isaiah had prophesied that Jesus would be a sanctuary. Yet, there was also the prophecy that Jesus would be "a stone of stumbling" and "a rock of offense" (Isaiah 8:14). Even today, Jesus is a stumbling block, an offense, to many people because their thinking just cannot grasp that there is only *one pathway to God*, and that pathway is Jesus Christ, the Word who became flesh and lived among men (John 1:14). They don't recognize that it is not God who "sends" people to a place of eternal punishment; it is individuals who make choices that result in eternal separation from God in a place the Bible calls hell.

In the Parable of the Sower, Jesus declared that people who receive the Word and are not rooted in it become offended when persecution or affliction arises *because of the Word:*

> And these are they likewise which are sown on stony ground; who, when they have heard the word, imme-diately receive it with gladness; And have no root in themselves, and so endure but for a time: afterward, when affliction or persecution ariseth for the word's sake, immediately they are offended. (Mark 4:16–17)

Jesus said people will allow the affliction or persecution that they face because of the Word to cause them to stumble. Not when they do something to deserve what they call persecution. Not because they are being disciplined or punished. But *because of the Word*. Jesus warned that the enemy of our souls will use persecution and oppression to cause us to lose the hope we have in the living Word and sever our relationship with God. We will become offended or turned aside from the truth if we are not firmly established in the truth, the Word of God. Eventually, I knew that those who become firmly established in God's Word will resist the kind of offense Jesus taught about.

As I thought about my friend's question, I asked myself, "Am I offended with God because of Lynn's death? Is God's Word choked out in my life because I didn't see the answer I wanted to see in my prayers for my son?"

At first, I leaned toward agreeing that I was offended. After mulling over that question for a few days and remembering the biblical use of the word, I decided I could not and would not allow myself to be offended with God. I would not allow what I was feeling to become offense. I had no desire to turn from God. I could admit that I had been angry with God at first; then, my anger had changed to disappointment. I was disappointed that God had seemingly not heard and answered my prayers for Lynn. I was crushed to think that my son might be in hell.

Even though I struggled with what had happened and my faith was sorely tested, I could not even think of giving up on God. I could not and would not let what happened to my son become a reason or excuse for abandoning my faith in God. Eventually, I came to the conclusion that my problem would not be offense. I could allow myself to grieve, but I would stick with God. I had come too far with Him to turn back now. And I realized that, once again, my faith was being stretched. I would allow God to take those painful circumstances and work them out to good.

I won't say that the process has been easy. Both Jim and I have had to keep strong our resolve to continue to trust God for answer to prayer. He has not failed us. He continues to surprise us. For one thing, He has brought circumstances into our lives that made Lynn's death and our family relationships with the woman who had been his wife and had given us two grandchildren, easier for Jim and me to deal with. First of all, she has been willing to allow us (maybe reluctantly at first) to continue as a part of her life. She must have sensed how much we loved her then and love her still. I hope that's the case. Second, even after marrying another man, she has trusted her babies to our care and allowed us to love on her like parents. Those babies call us Gran and Papa as if we were naturally related to them. It's a rare relationship for which we both thank God.

Strangely enough, God continued to work in another direction. Shortly after Lynn's death, my former daughter-in-law married again. Her new husband had already come into her life and the life of my grandchildren. He became willing to accept us into their lives. It must have been very awkward for him at first, but I think he learned to love us. We are so thankful that our grandchildren's stepfather loves the Lord, is a successful businessman and good provider, and willing to become a father figure to our then teenaged and preteen grandchildren. Finding normalcy for this new relationship was an arduous process for all of us, but Jim and I "adopted" him and are delighted to have this man of God, his parents, and his siblings in our lives. Both Jim and I feel so outrageously blessed that they are all part of our extended family. And God, most assuredly, has engineered the relationships. Our "adopted son" has endured many wisecracks because of his willingness to spend time with his wife's ex in-laws. We couldn't be happier and more thankful that he claims us anyway.

Would this relationship harmony ever have existed if we had allowed ourselves to become offended at God or anyone else involved in the matter? Since offense so often turns to bitterness and bitterness wreaks havoc with the health, both mental and physical, of those who are bitter; since bitterness causes people to "dry up on the vine," I'm sure our relationships would be different and much worse—if relationship had been possible at all.

The Bible cautions against bitterness in many places in the Old Testament as well as the New Testament. In Deuteronomy, Moses warns all of Israel to be careful that they allow no bitter root to grow up among them because it produces poison (Deuteronomy 29:18). In the New Testament, Paul commands that "all bitterness, and wrath, and anger, and clamour, and evil speaking, be put away from you, with all malice" (Ephesians 4:31). The Holy Spirit prompted him to point out that bitterness keeps company with evil, with unbridled anger and wickedness. These emotions are the antithesis of the fruit of the Spirit which Paul describes in Galatians (5:22–23): "love, joy, peace, longsuffering, gentleness, goodness, faith, Meekness, temperance."

And so, in the process called life, I have learned that all of our relationships—even our relationship with God—can be, and most likely will be, negatively affected when we allow ourselves to indulge in unforgiveness. If not dealt with promptly, if it grows and festers, it eventually becomes a root of bitterness. We guard against this root by keeping open lines of communication, by asking and giving forgiveness, by denying the right of all grievances—real or imagined—to continue in our minds. We replace such thoughts, instead, with verses from the Bible that encourage us to love, to forgive even as God forgives, and to pray for those who use and abuse us. During the Sermon on the Mount, Jesus said to His followers, "*Love* your enemies**, *bless*** them that curse you, *do good* to them that hate you, and *pray* for them which despitefully use you, and persecute you" (Matthew 5:44; emphasis added.) In Mark 11:25, He instructed, "And when ye stand praying, *forgive*, if ye have ought [anything] against any: that your Father also which is in heaven may forgive you your trespasses" (emphasis added). The Lord's command is serious. He will not forgive our sins if we don't forgive others who have sinned against us.

To guard against unforgiveness and bitterness, memorize and use those verses as the basis of your confessions. Then confess in prayer:

Lord, I love (my enemies and everyone else who has abused or misused me; call their names). I bless them and help them in any way I can. I ask you to do what I cannot; I ask you to change their lives and make them a witness for you. I ask you, also, to change me; make me a blessing to them somehow. I want to show them the same love and mercy you have shown me, and I will with your help. I pray this in the name of Jesus.

Father in heaven, I forgive (so and so) for (whatever he or she did to me). You know all about it, so I refuse, with your help and by your grace, to think on it. Instead, I make a conscious decision to act with intention. I refuse to harbor resentment and other thoughts and feelings that will keep you from forgiving me when I need it. I forgive. I bless. In the name of Jesus.

God has helped me to see that to forgive is not to forget, as popular myth suggests. Neither is it to cut yourself off from the offender. Some people claim to have forgiven, but then they refuse all association with those who have broken trust with them, misused them, or abused them or a family member. That attitude in my Christian friends and relatives concerns me. I pray for their spiritual well-being. I ask the Lord to open the eyes of their hearts, to give them understanding, to give them all-encompassing love.

Let's make the Lord Jesus our example. What if Jesus had said, "Father, I forgive those vile sinners, but I don't want to have anything to do with them. After all, I had to go through, isn't forgiveness enough? Do I really have to go and prepare a place for them to be with me throughout all eternity?" Think about it. No one has a better right to separate himself from those who take His name in vain; those who refuse to believe He is the way, the truth, and the life; those who worship at the altars of Mammon or other gods. Yet, Jesus is and always has been faithful. He can and will forgive every sin. Every sin, that is, except unbelief. Even Jesus Himself said, "*whosoever believeth* in him should not perish, but have eternal life (Matthew 3:15, emphasis added).

Yes, I said He forgives every sin but unbelief. What about blasphemy, you ask as you argue with my statement. Didn't Jesus Himself say we could be forgiven even if we blaspheme Him or God, but we would never be forgiven if we blaspheme the Holy Spirit? Let's read His words:

> "I tell you the truth, all sin and blasphemy can be forgiven, but anyone who blasphemes the Holy Spirit will never be forgiven. This is a sin with eternal consequences." He told them this because they were saying, "He's possessed by an evil spirit." (Mark 3:28–30 NLT; *see also* Luke 12:10)

In context, Jesus warns the Sadducees and the Pharisees to be careful what they say about the work of the Holy Spirit, also known as the Holy Ghost. They must guard against claiming that work done by the Spirit of God is work done by Satan. He specifies that all sins can be forgiven—even blasphemies against Him or anyone else—except for blasphemy of the Holy Spirit, an act which, as Jesus points out, puts the blasphemer "in danger of eternal damnation." Unpacking that Scripture helps to understand just what it means to blaspheme the Holy Spirit.

The Jewish dignitaries had just accused Jesus of healing by the power of Beelzebub, the devil. They *did not believe* in Jesus and His ability to free people from oppression. They *did not believe* that He was the promised Messiah. They *did not believe* that the power of God, the Holy Spirit, was at work through and by Him. Their unbelief led them to blasphemy, which means, generally, "defiant irreverence" (gotquestions.org/blasphemy-Holy-Spirit.html) or "to speak abusively or insultingly of someone or something" (biblestudytools.com/dictionaries/bakers-evangelical-dictionary/blasphemy-against-the-holy-spirit.html). They had hardened their hearts enough against the Son of God to claim that the specific work of the Holy Spirit through Jesus was a work of the devil. So to call the work of the Holy Spirit through Jesus or His disciples a work of the devil is to "blaspheme the Holy Spirit." The root of such blasphemy is a lack of faith in Jesus and the work He does or empowers believers to do by the power of the Holy Spirit. Anyone who makes such a statement is guilty of blasphemy, a sin that ultimately has its *roots in unbelief.*

Our mortal enemy has a huge bag of tricks. Offense and unbelief are only two of them. Refuse to allow Satan's work and his tricks to derail you and keep you from the best God has for you and the best you can give back to Him. You'll be amazed when you leave behind the works of the flesh like anger, wrath, bitterness, unforgiveness, malice, and such things. As you lean into Jesus for His help and strength, you'll experience unsurpassed love, gentleness, mercy, kindness, freedom, and peace through Him.

Chapter 16

MAKING DISCIPLES

Go then and make
disciples of all the nations.
–Matthew 28:19 AMP

———◆◆◆———

L ong before small groups became a big ministry in churches, Jim
and I led small groups.

In the late seventies, he led a group of teenagers, open to both boys
and girls, for almost four years. Most of the time only boys attended.
He provided short devotional sessions and played games with the
group. One time, long before the seatbelt laws went into effect, he
crammed all twelve of them plus himself into our Pinto station wagon
and took them to buy hamburgers. Jim poured himself into those young
people. They learned the Bible and had plenty of meaningful activities
and fellowship. They enjoyed themselves. They belonged.

As director of women's ministries in a small church, I had organized groups of praying women in our suburban church into three
groups according to where they lived in relation to the location of
the church. I was inspired that these were not to become "gossip sessions"; our goal was to meet to share Scripture and pray for needs of
the group and the church. We purposed to invite our unsaved relatives
and our neighbors who did not attend church anywhere. Any refresh-
ment served would be very simple and not bring hardship on the group
leaders. Knowing that God had inspired the groups, I plunged in and
led one of the groups myself. In retrospect, I realize that I should have
spent my time praying for, visiting, and encouraging the groups. The
groups were active, and active members claimed to feel blessed by

participating. However, not one group had unsaved friends or relatives to attend, including mine. But that fact slowed me down only a bit.

For several years, Jim and I helped to "pastor" a group of seniors at one church in Georgia. Without any training in small group ministry, we followed what we believed to be God's leading. In monthly meetings we enjoyed food, singing, and a short Bible lesson. We visited them when they were sick; we rejoiced with them at birthdays and weddings; we mourned with them and helped celebrate home goings of their family members. Since leaving the church where all of us were members, Jim and I have maintained a close relationship and an annual meeting with those people who made up the Senior Connection and are still part of our family of choice. We continue to love the people. We find that you don't stop loving those with whom you've worshipped for years after you know that God has led you somewhere else. We still feel a sense of responsibility for their spiritual and physical well-being.

Even after moving a few years ago to (as our pastor explains) a "church *of* small groups, not a church *with* small groups," we continue to lead small groups. For the most part, our devotional material or studies of the Bible at first came from previously published materials. We concluded that God had inspired and anointed the writers, and we could all benefit from their inspiration and anointing. And we did. Some of the most inspiring reading I have ever experienced became subjects of the small group studies we offered. Then came the time when I felt the Holy Spirit nudging me that we should expand our borders and seek our lesson material directly from Him and the Bible. I was supposed to write the curriculum. Another stretch, Lord? So, fighting anxiety and trembling, we began. To find inspiration for our group study or theme, we asked God to guide our search. All of the Scripture is good and profitable, but finding ways to bring its relevance to a changing world is the challenge as we look everywhere for ideas.

It's amazing how God has worked in such unexpected ways to turn up ideas. I'll share one example. While living on Lake Oconee, in Greensboro, Georgia, we began to receive regular newsletters from Skip Templeton, a realtor in Virginia. We'd never met him. How we ever got on his mailing list is a complete mystery, but I welcomed the newsletters. They were not the usual, run-of-the-mill, advertising pieces for his business, the kind that immediately goes into the round file. No, most of these carried inspiration and motivation. One in particular that

I tucked away in 2011 for later use is titled "Bend, Harden, or Blend." The title intrigued me; the material promised a kernel of inspiration.

Four or five years later, after moving twice, I was looking through boxes of papers I still had packed away. That one-page letter caught my eye again. There it was: "Bend, Harden, or Blend"!

Inspired to teach a short session on some of the tricks our adversary uses on Christian people and how we cope with the tricks, I was searching for a catchy title for that summer small group that would meet for six weeks. I found the words on the newsletter attention-getting, to say the least; maybe others would too. So I read the message again and pondered how it might apply to what we were inspired to teach. The ideas from the newsletter are always simple yet profound. This time the message went like this, short version:

> If you take an egg, a carrot, and coffee and drop them into boiling water, they react differently. Put a carrot into boiling water for a few minutes. When you bring it out, it will *bend*. Drop an egg into boiling water for a few minutes; it *hardens*. If you put ground coffee into boiling water, after a few minutes it *blends* with the water and turns it into something entirely new: a delectable beverage for coffee lovers.

The life application given in the letter was straightforward but secular; I was looking to give it a spiritual value.

So, I pondered the story and shared it with Jim, my husband and co-leader. We both liked it and discussed its merits for use with the summer's small group. How could we make this fit our purposes and goal for the summer session? Would it be a dud? Would people go away with unbiblical conclusions? We faced a quandary. The quandary was not bigger than God, so we looked to Him for direction. Again, He did not disappoint us!

Under the direction of the Holy Spirit and with Jim's encouragement, I submitted that title and a short blurb about the direction for the group to the online registry. The response was phenomenal. Twenty-seven people inquired and got directions. That would not be a "small group." It was more people than several small churches we have attended have on Sunday mornings. We weren't sure we could handle that many because we had no other location than our downsized home;

it was too late to find another venue. And we knew that very often several people have just shown up without inquiring or registering. Still, we were reluctant to turn people away.

At the first meeting, twenty-three people showed up. Our small group was no longer "small." Amazed and excited, we scrambled to find room for them in our smaller living-dining spaces and what architectural plans call an adjoining "rotunda" separated from the dining area by a large arch and little wall.

When we purchased the house just over five years ago, I lamented the wasted space of a rotunda that had only one usable wall—barely big enough for a double bookcase—and six openings into other rooms and the foyer. What did I know? God knew what He was doing when He directed us to look at the house. The rotunda was located at the end of the foyer and adjacent to the dining room through a large arch. Also opening into the living room, it could accommodate a five-foot round table with eight folding chairs. Our dining room seated eight. We could move furniture around in our living room and put in a rectangular table that would seat eight. So, with a few TV trays, we found enough space, and we enjoyed close encounters (pun intended) over the next six weeks.

What did we study?

That was part of our dilemma during this summer small group. We were going to examine how Christians should handle some common challenges in their lives. We all have situations that elicit a response from us. An angry argument with a spouse. A sibling "cheats" us out of something very special to us, and we want to get even. We don't get the job promotion that we had worked for so hard and long and looked forward to with great expectation. A younger, less experienced person seems to snatch it right from us. A loved one dies even though we pray the prayer of faith. We have choices about how to respond to these life challenges: we can bend under the load; we can harden our hearts against further hurt and disappointment. Or we can allow the Holy Spirit to cause the unhappy, the disappointing, the debilitating circumstances of life to stretch us to become a sweet-smelling sacrifice that pleases God.

Most of us face many situations that tempt us to hold grudges, harbor resentment, and allow bitterness to take root. From our own past experiences, Jim and I knew that the majority of us may have some measure of bitterness tucked away inside a secret place in our hearts.

So I went back to the Word. Warnings against bitterness abounded in the Old and New Testament. Paul cautions Christians to get rid of all bitterness and its accompanying anger and evil speaking (Ephesians 4:31). James (not my husband, the one in the Bible) warns that "bitter envying and strife in your hearts" (James 3:14) is of the devil, that such emotions lead to "confusion and every evil work" (James 3:16). Those verses settled it. I added a couple of inspirations from a delightful book, a favorite children's book I had run across almost twenty years ago. Written by Donna Perugini, it's called *Don't Hug a Grudge!* Then began an argument with myself. *Don't Hug a Grudge!* was written for children. Would a group of more than twenty adults whose ages ranged between twenty and sixty-something pay any attention to the message in a book written for children? Would they be offended?

I had dared to use the book to teach high school juniors and seniors during a state-mandated emphasis on character building. They had received the book with the usual veiled enthusiasm or utter nonchalance of young people their age. Would recent college graduates, young parents, and grandparents all in the same group respond positively?

That's one inspiration God gave us, so Jim and I took the leap of faith. We had about one hour to examine the progression of grudges that grow into resentment and eventually become bitterness.

I'd like to say that the day for that particular lesson came, and we entered into it with full confidence. That's not the case. I was still apprehensive, a bit like the cat on the hot tin roof. My temptation was to trust years of experience as a teacher. I knew I needed to rely on God. Fortunately, true to His promise to be a "very present help" (Psalm 46:1 KJV), the Spirit of God delivered.

Unable to seat the adults on the floor in a circle (most of them would not have been able to get back up again), I decided to read the story with the book open to the group. My "kids" were not only over-age; they were also over-sized. No floor for them. A cry for wisdom and favor sent heavenward started the session. I warned our group what to expect. They didn't seem to have an unfavorable reaction. So I plunged into the story.

All except one of the group listened eagerly and scanned the pictures as I walked among the three rooms open to each other and read from the pages—much the same way a teacher in a school setting with a large group of small children would have done. The only one who didn't attend closely was a cancer patient with a death sentence hanging over her head. A sudden onslaught of nausea captured her full attention. I could see that she was struggling. She made it to the end of the story and the Bible verses that gave it spiritual foundation. As she snaked her way through the crowded rooms to the restroom, we stopped what we were doing. The compassions of people who love God and His people with their whole hearts spilled into the room. One by one, this family of choice offered up prayers of faith for her healing and complete wholeness.

After that brief interlude, eyes sparkled and flashed as members of the group shared their perceptions of how grudges often grow into full-blown resentment. We examined the consequences to our mental and physical health when resentment festers until it bubbles up into bitterness, and bitterness is allowed to take root. The writer of Hebrews warns that bitterness causes deep trouble and defiles or hurts many in the process (Hebrews 12:15). The Word of God may have inspired many medical practitioners who recognize the illnesses, both physical and emotional, that result from rankling bitterness. I think our group got the message.

With boldness fueled by the positive reception of the children's book, we decided to delve into another challenge or temptation that trips up so many followers of Christ: judgment and hypocrisy. One of the well-known stories in the Gospels—that of the woman caught in the act of adultery—illustrates so powerfully how Jesus dealt with those who set themselves up to judge (John 8:1–11). So we took our group there to discover what we could learn from that episode. After all, we reminded ourselves, Scripture is given to provide a foundation for our belief system, to show us what we're doing wrong and how to do it right, and to instruct us in right living (2 Timothy 3:16).

As the story goes, Jesus is teaching in the temple where he is surrounded by people. Suddenly a group of lawyers and influential landowners who are master interpreters of the oral tradition, those known as scribes and Pharisees, interrupts his teaching. Dragging in a woman, they drop her at his feet. So they preempt Jesus. All eyes and minds suddenly shift their focus from the Giver of Life to the woman and her accusers who have stones in their hands.

As the experts in the law of Moses level the charge of adultery at her, they remind Jesus that the law instructs them to stone her. Desiring to trap Jesus, they demand to know what He says about the situation.

Without a word to them, Jesus stoops and starts writing on the ground. We questioned each other: "What did he write? Could it have been the names of those among them who had slept with her? The names of other women they might have had affairs with? A question about the whereabouts of the involved man that the law also condemns?"

The accusers don't let good enough alone. Continuing to pester Jesus, they finally hear His famous words, "Let the one who has not sinned cast the first stone."

One by one the men in the group drop their stones and slink out of the temple. After a charged silence, Jesus stands, faces the woman, and asks her, "Where are your accusers? Hasn't anyone condemned you?" With head still bowed, she answers, "No one, Lord."

With surprising gentleness and compassion, Jesus declares, "Neither do I condemn you. Go and sin no more."

Mercy speaks, "Go." Undeserved favor settles around the emotionally battered woman. Grace gives her a choice: "Sin no more."

Our group applied the message to their lives today. They agreed that Christians no longer use stones to condemn sin. Our favorite weapon today—our stones—are our words. We hear about a group of teens who wreck their car on the way home from a Friday night football game. Two of them die in the crash. The news outlets report that they had open containers of alcohol in the car. With little regard for the feelings of the grieving parents and friends, we sanctimoniously declare, "Well, they should not have been drinking!" It's a true statement, but what good does it do to point out the obvious after the fact? Where is the compassion for the families left behind?

In another instance, a young woman on a college campus is raped. Some old biddy in the neighborhood self-righteously observes, "She was asking for it the way she dressed. I've been saying that for years."

Are our "stones" any less lethal? The Word of God says that the words we speak spring from the overflow from our hearts (Matthew 12:34); sometimes, then, we spew unbelief, profanity, vulgarities. The origin? Our hearts, if we are to believe God's Word. The Bible also says that "the tongue can bring life or death" (Proverbs 18:21 NLT). We can destroy or bring life with the words we speak.

One version of a familiar story illustrates the concept of destructive words so well. This version involves a pastor and one of his members. This very popular pastor was serving the largest congregation in the area. He loved his sheep; they loved and honored him and his family.

The townspeople held him in the highest regard whether they were part of his congregation or not. By spreading rumors and innuendo, one of his members made it necessary for him to resign and may even have made it impossible for him to get another position as pastor anywhere else.

It seems that the member—I'll call her Mrs. Busy—spread rumors about something she thought she had witnessed involving the pastor and a widow who lived across the street from her. She didn't know it, but the pastor was consoling and helping the widow during the days surrounding her mother's death. As a result of Mrs. Busy's gossip, the pastor's reputation in the church and the community became tainted. Some of the deacons called for his resignation. Before he left the church, the pastor decided to confront her.

When Mrs. Busy learned of her misinterpretation and the truth behind what she saw, she reacted with shock and remorseful tears. After some minutes of crying, she asked the pastor what she could do to make restitution. He gave her a job.

He told her to take a down pillow to the highest point in the town, cut it open, and pour out all the feathers in the pillowcase. With relief flooding her face, she agreed to do that. Then, he added another step to the process. To make her restitution complete, she must then find every feather and replace it in the pillowcase. Astonishment and a fresh onslaught of tears followed his words. As she recognized the impossibility of the task, her soon to be ex-pastor warned her about the power of the tongue to destroy and to kill.

While this story may have no factual basis, it is a powerful story. It illustrates very well the power of the tongue to murder someone's reputation. Hopefully, we will think twice about what we think we're observing. Maybe we'll have the foresight to tell it only to God and let Him work out the situation.

Which do you choose? Will you bend, harden, or blend?

When you think about the circumstances you've encountered in your life, what would you say has been the outcome? Have you bent under the pressures? Have you hardened as a result of the heated circumstances? Or have you brought refreshing change to your environment? Have you been an agent of change for the better or have you allowed circumstances to turn your victory to defeat?

The choice is, always has been, and always will be *yours*!

What has been need not continue. You are not defined by your past. With Christ, you can stand tall and strong when the winds of adversity buffet you. When you find yourself in a fiery furnace—whether it's of your own making or not—you can expect the God of Shadrach, Meshach, and Abed-nego (Daniel 3:1–30) to be right there with you. He promised never to leave or forsake you (Hebrews 13:5), to be with you always. You will come out of the fire unscathed when you put your trust in the One who delivers. It is not the circumstances of life and the adversities that face us that make or break us. It is our response to those things. We can always choose how we respond. In anger or in love. In doubt or in confidence. In fear or in faith.

Choose love, confidence, and faith.

Chapter 17

HONORING WHEN HONOR IS NOT DUE

Honor thy father and thy mother.
–Exodus 20:12

————◦◉◦————

A s a child I learned early in life that disobedience and "talking back" would not be tolerated in my family. We girls never dared to question Dad or sass him. He ruled with a loving but firm demeanor that meant business. Occasionally, we let our mouth get out of control to Mom when Dad wasn't around. She was a bit more tolerant, but she disciplined us when she had reached her tolerance limit. Sometimes we received a whack with a belt or a spatula, but she never abused us. Both Mom and Dad walked in integrity (even though Dad's life was not exactly godly when his children were growing up) and thereby blessed their children (Proverbs 20:7).

They both followed the wisdom of the wisest king who ever lived. They knew that they must be careful to discipline their children if they loved them (Proverbs 13:24). Solomon also advised, "The rod and reproof give wisdom, But a child left to himself brings shame" (Proverbs 29:15 NKJV). Mom and Dad were not like many modern parents who want to be their children's friends. Their job, once the first child was born, and as they saw it, was to be parents to those they brought into this world. They believed children needed to obey, to learn good manners, to respect authority, and to work hard to achieve goals—their own and those of the family. They also loved the other children in the family—nieces, nephews, grandchildren—enough to discipline them while the children were in their care. As a result of their parenting, they taught my sisters and me early in life that they expected their children to be obedient, to be seen, and to be heard as long as we were respectful in our choice of words and our tone of voice.

By their teaching and their example both Mom and Dad taught us what it means to honor their parents. My dad's dad lived in our house most of Mom and Dad's married life. He suffered from emphysema and was unable to work. Even though his strong will and unpopular opinions created great tension between him and Mom, she cared for him when he was sick just as she cared for her parents. When he passed away, Mom took care of her mother and then brought her mother's sister to her house. She gave both of them first-rate care until they breathed their last breath. My parents practiced the commandment that promised a conditional longevity: "Honor thy father and mother; (which is the first commandment with promise;) That it may be well with thee, and thou mayest live long on the earth" (Ephesians 6:2–3; *see also* Exodus 20:12).

A promise of long life. It's something that most of us hope for. So, based on Scripture and on the desire to live long and strong, what does it mean to "honor" our parents? If we want to benefit from that Scriptural promise, we certainly want to know. And then, once we know, we sometimes must put all our strength into the s-t-r-e-t-c-h to be eligible for the promise.

Webster defines *honor* as "esteem due or paid to worth; high estimation; respect; consideration; manifestation of respect or reverence." From this definition, we can safely conclude that the Bible admonishes us to esteem our parents, to hold them in high regard, to give them the consideration due their position as the people who gave birth to us. Pastor Ray Kirkland (Family Worship Center, Beckley, WV) declares that "honor is not about keeping a bunch of rules; it is not earned. Respect is earned. Honor is appointed." I agree with him.

The Bible does not give anyone license to rebel against or curse or speak disrespectfully to or about our parents no matter what they have or have not done. But, you may protest, what if the circumstances of your life with your parents or without them seem to suggest or prove outright that they don't deserve your honor or respect? I've asked myself that question many times. I've taken the matter to God in prayer. I put it on my "shelf" to be contemplated with a promise to seek for answers later. It was not until I understood God's grace, his undeserved mercy and favor, that I have been able to find answers to that question and many others.

The Bible also doesn't overtly handle all the "what ifs" of life. What if the parent is verbally or physically or sexually abusive? What if the parent abuses alcohol or drugs and spends on an addiction the money the family needs for living? What if the parent(s) deserted the child? The admonition to honor is not qualified; it is not conditioned upon parental behavior. It is a command. So, some of us may find ourselves crying out to God:

> Dear God. You sometimes command us to do things that we just cannot do. How can You expect a child to love and honor a father who abused her sexually from the time she was old enough to remember? How can a child love biological parents who deserted him when he was just a baby? How can that grown man love a father who maimed him physically through drunken anger and rage?

If I can paraphrase a bit, God answers the cry: "I love you. I loved you and those who abused you even when you were all sinners. A sin is a sin. I don't label sins and put them in a hierarchy with some being worse than others. Everyone has sinned and comes short of the glory of God. With me all things are possible. Just go ahead and stretch. I'll give you the grace to forgive and love to replace the bitterness you feel."

God's promise is not just to people who live in Israel or the United States of America. It is a promise to all who receive Jesus as Savior and Lord, to all those who *receive* and *believe* God's Word. Some people that we ministered to in Peru, both victims and perpetrators, confronted God's Word about what had happened to or through them.

A Rescue Mission

Our first of two mission trips to Peru left Jim and me with many memories, some of which had to do with parenting and living conditions. One thing I remember most about that first trip was a small village just outside Lima with a heavenly name. I'll call it Celestial City to protect the anonymity of the residents. Celestial City was built on the side of the dustiest mountain I have ever seen. I want to call it a village, but maybe the term "village" suggests too organized a space. This area was really a conglomeration of the crudest makeshift huts constructed of whatever materials a family could salvage from the ravages of a war-torn country: cardboard, stones, cement blocks. Often they were topped with a large piece of corrugated tin held to the structure with a sizable rock at each of four corners and floored with tamped-down dirt.

The "homes" sat wherever families could find or dig out a rock or a ledge big enough to hold just one room, often no more than nine feet by nine feet, smaller than many walk-in closets in the US. Of course, these homes had no running water, no toilets, no sanitation system whatsoever. Large water tankers delivered water to communal barrels daily, and women and children carried buckets of water up the somewhat treacherous paths to their kitchens or clothes washing tubs. A single light bulb dangled from a single wire attached to the main room ceiling. It was the kind of lighting that prevailed in the homes of the area in which I lived during my childhood. The living conditions in Celestial City and other small residential areas resulted from abject poverty and the chaos of a country that had just experienced an internal revolution against what they considered a corrupt government.

On the streets to this small "village" and in the nearby city, rubble from destroyed buildings and streets marred the landscape. Even though the rubble was neatly piled up, the piles held sidewalks, buildings, and open lots hostage. Transportation was possible, but streets were barely freed of the aftermath of war. Many businesses were still closed, and many men and women had no work to sustain them and their families beyond a mere existence level. Hopelessness seemed to have gripped the majority of the population, especially the men.

The small huts on the hillsides and mountains were home to single families—no matter how large the family was. The pastor of a church that served Celestial City invited us to a prayer service there. It was held in a small hut larger than most with two rooms located at the top of a steep rock stairway about half way up the mountain. After a hard climb of 500 to 750 feet, almost straight up, we reached the hut. The family had moved all the furniture, meager as it was, out of the room we met in and placed a few once-white plastic picnic chairs at the front of the bare room. They had invited their neighbors to a worship service with preaching to follow.

Along with the chairs, one large amplifier, a microphone on a stand, and a drum furnished the room. The people considered the five visitors, including the two US pastors who led the mission trip, our host pastor, Jim, and me honored guests. They expected us to take the plastic seats of honor. Winded from unaccustomed strenuous activity, I was glad to do so. About twenty to fifty people stood around the room and just outside the door. We only glimpsed the second room—a kitchen. It was much smaller than the living/sleeping room. As I recall, we learned that a family of twelve lived there. We made a joyful noise as we worshiped the Lord and heard words of scriptural encouragement from the pastors whom we accompanied to Peru.

Many other homes were smaller—more often only one room. As far as we knew, none of them had inside plumbing. Furnishings, such as they were, were sparse and well-worn. But a surprising number of the homes had a tiny TV set stationed on a cinderblock or some kind of makeshift structure even if the home had only one room. It was connected with the one bulb in the ceiling and sported the proverbial "rabbit ears" antenna. No plush couches and chairs graced the room. Tired parents had no footstools on which to prop their feet. No comfortable beds welcomed the family at night.

Such a cramped space made no room for privacy. The host pastor shared with us that incest was rampant, that fathers and brothers and uncles freely ravaged their daughters, sisters, or nieces. More often than not, the men were drunk in their hopelessness. Somehow, they always managed to find enough money for liquor. Does that excuse their behavior? Certainly not! It might just be one explanation for what happens in lives everywhere when the enemy of their souls tells them, "There is no hope; no one cares; if there's a God, even He doesn't care."

So, what were the girls to do? They had no one to tell. No Department of Family and Children's Services helped them to get away from their nightmares. What about the wives and mothers and aunts who must have been privy to what was going on under the roof of their very small space? How do we teach those who have been abused to love the abuser? To love and honor the mothers who turn a blind eye to what they feel powerless to stop? To forgive those who stole their innocence and put them through hell on earth?

No one can achieve that kind of forgiveness without God's help. No one. The average wage then was, in US dollars, about $500 per year. Even the starting pay for teachers was just $1800 per year. Poverty prevailed among those we ministered to in Peru, so they couldn't afford psychological intervention even if they had considered it. But we believed then and continue to believe that God can turn a mess into a message; with Him all things *are* possible. Jim and I prayed to help them find a way to forgiveness and peace. We knew that the abused as well as the abusers had to know that Someone loves them. They needed to hear that God loves them so much that He provided a way to give them hope, help, and healing. We could and did teach them that God is love, that He loved so much that He was willing to send Jesus to die for the sins of everyone, the girls and their abusers alike. Jesus was willing to die on a crude cross to pay the abusers' sin debt and set them free. Many of them prayed to receive the help that God offered.

The love of Father God working in and through the abused allows them to love again. Receiving His love enables them to feel secure again. Prayer and faith in a loving God, a faith nurtured by immersion into the Word of God, works miracles. Those are the ingredients that help the abused to allow forgiveness to flow and a root of bitterness to be uprooted from their hearts so that they can heal and move on. They simply must embrace the forgiveness. They must forgive.

That's the same prescription for the abuser. Their repentance by faith and God's work in them allow the abusers to free themselves from their past, to know that their past no longer identifies them. Even those who have abused their daughters, nieces, and granddaughters as well as those who have abused their sons, nephews, and grandsons can be set free from the bondage of their sins and degradation. Scripture teaches that "God so loved the world" (John 3:16). That "world" includes the pedophile, the pervert, other sex offenders, the murderer, the addict, the thief, the atheist, the agnostic. He loved every person so much that He gave His Son Jesus to die on the cross to pay the debts for all sins—past, present, and future. With the past behind them, they are no longer defined by what the blood of Jesus has washed away. Like other sinners, the abusers must also forgive themselves.

The same love that cleanses and brings healing to the abused also offers the abuser forgiveness, love, hope, and new life. The human way is to punish forever. But God.

But God. I love that interruption we often see in Scripture. *But God.* God is different. His way is to forgive the repentant and cleanse them. His way is to help the abused to forgive. Such forgiveness is not possible by human will alone; it takes the help of the Holy Spirit of God, also known as the Comforter and "the Spirit of truth," Jesus promised would be available to believers once He ascended back to the Father after His resurrection (John 14:16 and 16:7–8, 13). We receive the person known as the Holy Spirit, and His work in our lives the same way we receive the forgiveness of our sins: by faith.

Healing the Hurt

Most of the time, we want to punish those who hurt us, so we withhold our forgiveness. But an unforgiving spirit toward them does not hurt the defilers; it hurts the one clinging to unforgiveness. Eventually, it turns into a root of bitterness in the one defiled. That bitterness, left unchecked, destroys from within. It crowds out love, mercy, grace, peace—all the attributes of God that became ours when we gave our hearts to him. The only way to eradicate bitterness is to forgive. Is it easy? Not by a long shot! Is it possible? Yes. God makes it possible.

Besides teaching us to honor father and mother, God's Word also insists that we treat others the way we would like to be treated, to turn the other cheek, to love the unlovely (Luke 6:31; Matthew 5:39)—the absent parents, the pedophiles, the perverts, the murderers, the sex offenders, the drug lords who peddle disaster to our young people; the terrorists who rape, murder, pillage, and destroy.

Don't expect that behavior to be easy. It will not be.

Is it possible? I believe it is. But only if we know and accept who we are in Christ.

Who Am I? Who Are You?

Over and over again, I've heard well-meaning Christian people, including pastors, proclaiming:

"I'm just an old sinner saved by grace."

"I'm just a dirt bag."

"I'm a nobody."

Such proclamations have a sound of humility, but I suggest that they're far from humble. In the light of God's Word, those statements are really arrogant. Even more arrogant than to claim, "I'm Somebody. Who are you? Are you Somebody too?" (Remember that nod to Emily Dickinson?) The arrogance is all wrapped up in a show of "fake" or unfounded humility. People who use such statements may truly not know what the Bible has to say about them. Or they have the audacity to deny what God's Word says. Please allow me to explain.

Let's agree up front to take the Bible as our truth, our proof of who we are. The Bible plainly says, "For all have sinned and come short of the glory of God" (Romans 3:23). That says *all*. You, me, everyone else who has ever lived or whoever will live. No exceptions. So someone who sins is a sinner? That Bible verse seems to lend credence to the "old sinner saved by grace" statement. But does it?

After his conversion, Paul declares, "If any man be in Christ, he is a *new creature*: old things are passed away; behold, all things are become new" (2 Corinthians 5:17, emphasis added). He goes on to assure believers that God has reconciled us to Himself by Jesus Christ, the only perfect sacrifice, the One who became "sin for us . . . that we might be made the righteousness of God in him" (2 Corinthians 5:21). It is because of Christ's payment for our sins on the cross that God no longer counts our sins against us. He no longer sees the people who have repented and committed their lives to Christ as sinners. He sees us as brand *new creations. Paul says that the person who is "joined to the Lord is one spirit with him"* (1 Corinthians 6:17 NLT).

God no longer counts the sins of those of us who receive Christ as Savior against us. The thought is mind boggling. It requires and inspires meditation. You and I have sinned and continue to miss the mark, but God no longer counts our sins against us. Since God's inspired Word, penned by Paul, calls us the righteousness of God in Christ, then it is totally inappropriate to call ourselves "dirt bags" and "old sinners."

Paul asserts that if we have to work for our salvation, we are getting wages instead of a reward because God would owe us. If we don't have to work to earn our salvation but need only to put our full trust and reliance in the One who justifies us while we're ungodly, our faith is considered righteousness (Romans 4:4–5), and we become the righteousness of God. Paul refers specifically to a Psalm of David when he says: "Blessed are those whose iniquities are forgiven, and whose sins are covered. Blessed is the man to whom the Lord will not impute sin" (Psalm 32:1–2; Romans 4:7–8).

Impute, according to Merriam-Webster, means "to credit to a person or a cause." In the KJV Dictionary, it is defined as "to charge or accuse." That it's possible for you or me to be a person to whom the Lord God will not impute sin seems unreal. The definitions, however, help us to understand that when God forgives our sins, he no longer charges our sins to our account or accuses us of sin. Others might. We might. God does not. Another bonus here is God's assurance that He will drive all

171

our sins "into the depths of the seas" (Micah 7:19). In other words, He puts them completely out of His mind; it is as if they never existed.

God is not a dirt bag. God is not a nobody. God is not an old sinner. Even Jesus, God in the flesh, who came to this earth and lived as a man, never gave in to the temptation of sin. If we're one spirit with Him, we have become new creations—new people who have never existed before on this earth. Same body, same soul; brand-new spirit. Changed where it counts. It is inappropriate to call ourselves sinners. Because we're still human and continue to have issues with human appetites, because we constantly have to bring our fleshly appetites under control of the Holy Spirit, we may fail to measure up to God's standard from time to time. However, God does not count those failures against us. He does not count your failures against you if you're a believer. He has called you righteous. According to the King James Version Dictionary meaning of *righteous*, God has called you "holy in heart, and observant of the divine commands in practice." Another widely used understanding of the word is that the righteous are "in right standing with God."

Paul exhorts believers that there is no condemnation to those *in Christ* Jesus (Romans 8:1). Then he explains what it means to be in Christ: "But ye are not in the flesh, but in the Spirit, if . . . the Spirit of God dwell in you" (Romans 8:9). He continues, "If thou shalt confess with thy mouth the Lord Jesus. and shalt believe in thine heart that God hath raised him from the dead, thou shalt be saved" (Romans 10:9). He also assures that "whosoever shall call upon the name of the Lord shall be saved" (Romans 10:13). According to Paul, to be saved is to live and walk according to the leading of the Spirit; it is to be in Christ (Romans 8:1). For you and me, once we give our hearts to the Lord and confess Him as Lord and Savior, we are in Christ, and "in Him we live, and move, and have our being" (Acts 17:28).

To be in Him is not a complicated process. You begin reaching toward that goal when you decide to recognize and accept that you are a sinner, that you need a Savior. The next step is your step of faith: believe and accept that Jesus took the sins of the world on Himself and died on the cross for everyone's sins—even your sins—and that He defeated death when He was resurrected from the dead. You achieve being in Christ when you repent (change your mind about how to live, turn around, and leave your life of sin), when you dedicate yourself to learning about and living a God-first life, when you use Him as your example and walk according to His moral code. In other words, you die to self and allow Him to raise you to new life. Paul calls that step in your walk with God being "buried with him by baptism unto death" and raised to newness of life. He says it this way: "In whom [Christ] we have redemption through his blood, the forgiveness of sins, according to the riches of his grace" (Ephesians 1:7). In Romans 6:3–18 Paul urges believers:

> Know ye not, that so many of us as were baptized into Jesus Christ were baptized into his death? Therefore we are buried with him by baptism into death: that like as Christ was raised up from the dead by the glory of the Father, even so we also should walk in newness of life. For if we have been planted together in the likeness of his death, we shall be also in the likeness of his resurrection: Knowing this, that our old man is crucified with him, that the body of sin might be destroyed, that henceforth we should not serve sin. For he that is dead is freed from sin.

> Now if we be dead with Christ, we believe that we shall also live with him: Knowing that Christ being raised from the dead dieth no more; death hath no more dominion over him. For in that he died, he died unto sin once: but in that he liveth, he liveth unto God. Likewise reckon ye also yourselves to be dead indeed unto sin, but alive unto God through Jesus Christ our Lord. Let not sin therefore reign in your mortal body, that ye should obey it in the lusts thereof. Neither yield ye your members as instruments of unrighteousness unto sin: but yield yourselves unto God, as those that are alive from the dead, and your members [all parts of your bodies] as instruments of righteousness unto God.

> For sin shall not have dominion over you: for ye are not under the law, but under grace. What then? shall we sin, because we are not under the law, but under grace? God forbid. Know ye not, that to whom ye yield

yourselves servants to obey, his servants ye are to whom ye obey; whether of sin unto death, or of obedience unto righteousness? But God be thanked, that ye were the servants of sin, but ye have obeyed from the heart that form of doctrine which was delivered you. *Being then made free from sin*, ye became the servants of righteousness (emphasis added).

In one short chapter of the New Testament, Paul describes many of the characteristics and benefits of the believer, the one who is *in Christ*. According to Romans 6, it doesn't matter who you are or what you've done. The moment you accept Christ as your Savior, you possess, among many other benefits, resurrection power (v. 5). In addition, you are

Crucified with Christ (v. 6);
Freed from sin (v.7);
Dead with Christ and able to live with Him (v. 8);
Dead to sin and alive unto God (vv. 9–10);
Under grace, his undeserved and unearned favor (v. 14);
Slaves to righteous living (v. 18).

Who Am I And Who Are You, Scripturally Speaking?

The Bible enumerates many promises about who believers are and what they can expect from God once they become born again, once they become those new creations Paul describes. While all of them are important, they are too numerous to list and comment on each one of them here. By the ones I have chosen, I hope to give you a head start in terms of being able to rebuff the temptations to demean and downgrade yourselves or to allow your enemy to do so. Like Christ when Satan came to Him in the wilderness, we, too, can be armed with the powerful ammunition: "It is written." A careful knowledge of the following will enable you in two areas. For one thing, it will equip you so that you don't deny what God has already said about you. It will also help you to be able to use the Sword of the Spirit, the powerful Word of God, to defeat your enemy on the battlefield of your mind.

You are a child of the Most High God and Co-Heirs with Jesus.

The Holy Spirit inspired both John and Paul with this assurance. John says, "But as many as received him, to them gave he power to become the sons of God, even to them that believe on his name" (John 1:12).

Paul continues the teaching and adds another dimension as he instructs believers everywhere that "thou art no more a servant, but a son; and if a son, then an heir of God through Christ" (Galatians 4:7). He continues the thought in another letter: "The Spirit [himself] beareth witness with our spirit, that we are the children of God: And if children, then heirs; heirs of God, and joint-heirs with Christ" (Roman 8:16–17).

Believers led by the Spirit of God are children of God; they qualify to inherit all that belongs to Christ (Romans 8:14–17). That promise is ours today. Heirs and joint heirs or co-heirs with Christ have a title deed to all that Christ has; they are able to enjoy all that is His. It sounds too good to be true. It is too good to be true—without Jesus Christ. It is a promise of God to those who are *in Christ*. Remember, all the promises of God in Christ are yes and amen (2 Corinthians 1:20). They are not, as they were under the Old Covenant (the Mosaic Covenant), "If you do this, then I'll do that."

You are not a servant of sin; you are a servant of righteousness, delivered from the power of darkness. (Romans 6:18)

After assuring us that "sin shall not have dominion" over us, Paul warns us not to let sin control our bodies (Romans 6:12, 14) and gives us other promises: "Being then made free from sin, ye became the servants of righteousness" (Romans 6:18). He also promises that "[God] hath delivered us from the power of darkness, and hath translated us into the kingdom of his dear Son: In whom we have redemption through his blood, even the forgiveness of sins" (Colossians 1:13–14).

You are a member of the body of Christ, placed in the body as the Lord chooses.

As a servant of righteousness and one who overcomes the attraction and appeal of sin, we are prepared to take our place in the church, the body of Christ: "Now ye are the body of Christ, and members in particular" (1 Corinthians 12:27). Known metaphorically as members in particular of the body of Christ, we have no choice of which body part to assume: the eyes or the ears or the hands or the feet or any other part. God places us in the body where He wants us, and we have the privilege to function there in the way for which He has designed us.

Besides being a member of Christ's body, you and I are so much more—if we've given our lives to Christ. The Word of God declares:

You are an overcomer!

John the apostle, one of the Lord's inner circle, encourages followers of Jesus to know that they "have [already is implied] overcome" every spirit that is not of God (1 John 2:13). The verb form "have overcome," in English, speaks of an action that began in the past and continues into the present. In the same vein of assuring continuing victory in steadfastness and consistency, John also says, "Whatsoever is born of God overcometh the world: and this is the victory that overcometh the world, even our faith. Who is he that overcometh the world, but he that believeth that Jesus is the Son of God?" (1 John 5:4–5)

Our faith in faithful God assures that we have what it takes to continue victoriously our life in Christ.

You are victorious, a conqueror.

Neither trials, nor stresses of daily living, nor wars, nor loss of life; none of the challenges and perils of life can separate us from God's love. Paul declares, "In all these things we are more than conquerors through him that loved us" (Romans 8:37), because it is God who "giveth [gives and keeps on giving] us the victory through our Lord Jesus Christ" (1 Corinthians 15:57).

You are the dwelling place of the Holy Spirit.

Before His crucifixion, Jesus speaks of His going away. He tells His disciples then and, by extension, those of us who would become his disciples in the future:

And I will pray the Father, and he shall give you another
Comforter, that he may abide with you forever; Even

the Spirit of truth; whom the world cannot receive, because it seeth him not, neither knoweth him: but ye know him; for he dwelleth with you, and *shall be in you* (John 14:16–17; emphasis added).

Writing after the day of Pentecost when the Holy Spirit fell upon the disciples gathered in the upper room, Paul challenges believers who had received the Spirit baptism: "Know ye not that your body is the temple of the *Holy Ghost which is in you* . . . and ye are not your own?" (1 Corinthians 6:19; emphasis added).

Consider just how powerful the promises of Jesus are, both as He spoke them and as He inspired Paul and others to write them. When you feel that your prayers are bouncing back from a closed heaven, when it seems that they have reached no farther than the ceiling, consider this: They do not have to go anywhere. The Spirit of the Living God has taken up residence inside the believers who have received Christ as their Lord and Savior. He is not far away and hard of hearing. He is even nearer than a whisper.

You are an ambassador with authority and power.

Over the years, people in the US and elsewhere have learned to honor and respect individuals whom their president or other governing official named as ambassadors. These appointed individuals officially represent the president or ruler and their country in other countries. Jesus has named those who follow Him as His ambassadors or representatives and empowered them to do His work on earth:

> And Jesus came and spake unto them, saying, All power is given unto me in heaven and in earth. Go ye therefore, and teach all nations, baptizing them in the name of the Father, and of the Son, and of the Holy Ghost: Teaching them to observe all things whatsoever I have commanded you: and, lo, I am with you always, even unto the end of the world. Amen. (Matthew 28:18–20)

Mark continues with the authority given to those ambassadors:

> And these *signs shall follow them that believe*; In my
> name shall they cast out devils; they shall speak with
> new tongues; They shall take up serpents; and if they
> drink any deadly thing, it shall not hurt them; they shall
> lay hands on the sick, and they shall recover (Mark
> 16:17–18, emphasis added).

Did you focus on all the things believers—yes, even you—are now commanded and empowered to do? After noting, according to Matthew, that Jesus has all power in heaven and in earth, we observe the word *therefore*. I don't think it was used carelessly; I think it's intentional. When we read "therefore," we know it means "for that reason." Because He has the power and authority to do so, He commands those who follow Him to accomplish certain things that He started on the earth. In effect, He makes us His ambassadors as He gives the power and authority "to go, teach, baptize, cast out devils, speak with new tongues." He also gives the ability, but not the command, to handle serpents or drink something deadly without harm. Then he instructs disciples past and present, "Lay hands on the sick who will subsequently be well."

Why would anyone with the power and authority to do these wonders in the name (the power and the authority) of Jesus want to hang his or her head and declare, "I'm just an old dirt bag"? I suggest it may be because we don't know any better; it may also be because we want to sound humble, but we contradict the Lord when we do so.

You are special in multiple ways.

You are a "chosen generation, a royal priesthood, an holy nation, a peculiar [God's own special] people . . . called . . . out of darkness into his marvellous light." (1 Peter 2:9)

Blessed be the God and Father of our Lord Jesus Christ, who hath blessed us with all spiritual blessings in heavenly places in Christ . . . he hath chosen us in him before the foundation of the world . . . [to] be holy and without blame before him . . . Having predestinated us unto the adoption of children by Jesus Christ . . . he hath made us accepted in the beloved . . . In whom we have redemption through his blood, the forgiveness of sins, according to the riches of his grace; Wherein he hath abounded toward us in all wisdom and prudence; Having made known unto us the mystery of his will. (Ephesians 1:3–9)

I've finally learned that when you know who you are, then you'll live like who you are. But you first have to be convinced of who you are. You have to stop listening to the chatterbox between your ears or the beguiling voice on your shoulder and start listening to the Words of the Creator of the universe. The best thing you can do is to live out what God has said about you. Start with your thinking. Straighten out your thinking about who you are by meditating on what God says. Then you will speak the right words—God's words—about who you are, not arrogantly but humbly and with thanksgiving. As you become convinced of who you are in Christ, you'll want to live it out. Your right thinking leads to right speaking; right speaking leads to right actions, and, in those right actions, you will find your destiny; you will fulfill the role that you are destined to fill as a "member in particular" of the body of Christ.

Today, stop to think about who God says you are—in Christ. You will find what His Word says captivating. Hopefully, you will have the eyes of your heart opened and enlightened and not take as long as I did to be blessed with knowledge that threatens to take your breath away. It will encourage you to be all He has arranged and planned for you to be, to be stretched beyond the limits of who you are in yourself and become the embodiment of who His Word says you are. What and who you are in Christ. When you and I stop doing life our way, learn from His Word what His will is and submit to it, we will become who He meant us to be; we will fulfill *His* vision for us.

Can we become all we are meant to be by ourselves? Many famous, wealthy, and influential people have never accepted Christ as their personal Lord and Savior. In their minds and words, they consider their own accomplishments a result, as my dad used to say, of "lifting themselves up by their own bootstraps." Many of them say they don't need a Savior. Others claim, like one of the successful authors of fiction I once read, that faith in a risen Savior is a "crutch" weak people need and rely on. On the other hand, an innumerable host of people on this earth have either not yet heard about the plans, promises, and provisions that God has for all people, or they have turned their backs on Him. Do these people and their circumstances make void what the Scriptures say? That's a question each individual confronted with the gospel must answer. Each of us must decide whether to listen to "reason" or to believe what the Bible says.

In Ephesians 3:16–19 we find Paul's prayer that God would strengthen believers "with might by his Spirit in the inner man; That Christ may dwell in [their] hearts by faith; that [they might be] rooted and grounded in love . . . and filled with all the fullness of God" (Ephesians 3:16–19). He also encourages believers everywhere to *"be strong in the Lord, and in the power of His might"* (Ephesians 6:10, emphasis added).

It is only in Christ that we are able to fulfill God's plan for our lives and accomplish His purposes. Without Jesus Christ, we will never be totally satisfied with our achievements. Without Him, we will never be able to fill the God-sized void in our lives as we search for fulfillment and inner peace.

The bottom line, then, is this: those who place their faith in Jesus Christ and walk in newness of life get right standing with God and no longer need to fear His judgment. This truth is something that has taken me a lifetime to receive because of early religious training with its emphasis on traditions and what some call "sin consciousness." I'm thankful that because of God's patient and merciful teaching and encouragement I am no longer a slave to legalism. I have finally discovered what it means to be "grace conscious."

Chapter 18

ON CHOOSING

Two roads diverged in a wood, and I—
I took the one less traveled by,
And that has made all the difference.
—Robert Frost, from "The Road Less Traveled"

———◦———

A t what stage in life do people begin to look back and ponder what might have been? Does anyone live who has never considered how changed their lives might be if they had made a different choice—a different school, a different career, a different spouse, a different neighborhood, a different church? These kinds of thoughts can paralyze, or they can launch.

It seems just as true with Christians as with those who have not joined the ranks of believers. The person who accepts Christ as Savior and Lord can expect the Lord to provide the navigation for his life journey; the psalmist says He will order our steps (Psalm 37:23). In fact, the Bible also says that God is at work within you, giving you the will and the power to achieve his purpose (Philippians 2:13). It's refreshing and empowering to know that we don't have to go forward in our own willpower. The will to do God's will comes from Almighty God Himself. Then, after He has given us a plan and a will to do it, He infuses us with the power and authority to accomplish it (Luke 9:1).

As we have seen in Scripture, it is He who supplies everything we need (Philippians 4:13).

On the authority of the Bible, we can conclude that God has a purpose for our lives, and it is He who gives us ideas and helps us bring those ideas to reality. What a thought—that the God of the universe, the Creator, is interested enough in the affairs of individuals that He is willing to plant dreams and provide the GPS (God-Powered System) to realize those dreams. Why do we then reach back into memory for decisions to second guess?

How does it happen? Perhaps God's ideas and purposes for our lives get tangled in our own dreams and aspirations. Perhaps, like kudzu, the menace of Southern trees and shrubbery, forces in our lives completely choke out what He planted. Do we get an idea from Him and then llow doubts to overwhelm us?

"I can't do that; I don't have the money to pursue several years of education."

"I'm too old."

"I'm not smart enough."

"I come from the wrong background; I don't have the right kind of contacts."

"I've never been self-disciplined. My life has been one big lump of unrealized dreams, of unfinished projects. What makes me think this would be any different?"

Calling ourselves realists, we often bury God-given dreams and desires because our faith is puny or overwhelmed by doubt. Or it fails us midstream. Unwilling to get in God's wheelbarrow and cross Niagara Falls with Jesus Himself navigating the tightrope, we settle for what Pastor Steven Furtick in his book *Greater* calls "the lesser." This willingness to settle for less than God's best becomes increasingly easy as we age. The culture of the US is not kind to the aged. Even in the church, sometimes people's talents and gifts are overlooked or over-shadowed; because they're not young any longer, they are seen as "old" and unproductive. Perhaps they even tag themselves with those labels.

Maybe, we are more like Peter than we want to admit. Just after Christ used the disciples—including Peter—to help Him feed 5,000 men (not counting possibly 10,000 or more women and children) with a two-piece lunch from Captain D's (modern version), He urges His disciples to get in the boat and go to the other side of the sea of Galilee while He stays where He is to pray a while. He promises to join them later. Why does He have to urge them? Do they see with their natural eyes something that causes them to hesitate? Do their experiences on the sea warn them to be cautious?

Possibly recognizing all the signs of an impending storm, the faithful followers reluctantly obey Him, and a storm meets them along the way. Wind and waves rock their boat and threaten to swamp the small craft. The grown men, some of them experienced fishermen, cower in fear for their lives.

Overwhelmed with panic, they spy a figure of a man walking toward them on the water. What they think is a "spirit" terrifies them. Sensing their fear, Jesus calls out to them:

"It is I; be not afraid."

Impetuous Peter speaks to the "spirit."

"If it's you, Lord, tell me to come to you."

Just wanted to be certain not to respond to an alien voice?

"Come."

One word. An invitation? A command? Peter hears His voice. He recognizes the Master's voice, responds in faith, and moves far out of his comfort zone. A few breaths later, he finds himself out of the boat and walking toward Jesus. Was he walking on the water, or was he walking on his faith? Some have claimed He was walking on the Word. The Bible says he "*walked on water.*" The important thing is, his faith powers his climb over the side of the boat and onto the waves that had, just moments before, nearly paralyzed him with fear.

So Peter walks on a stormy sea toward Jesus. As long as He keeps His eyes on the Lord, Peter defies natural laws. He is able to do the impossible. In the same way, Jesus often empowers us to do what we might have believed impossible — start a new business, learn to speak a foreign language, finish high school as an adult, play a musical instrument, lead a small group, leave our church of forty years and allow Him to plant us where He leads. Like the psalmist, when we find where our ability comes from, we learn that we can "run through a troup" or "leap over a wall" (Psalm 18:29); we can be sure that our help and our ability come from the Lord (Psalm 63:7 and Psalm 121:1).

It is not until Peter takes His eyes off Jesus and looks around at his circumstances (the winds and tossing waves) that his faith fails him. He begins to sink (Matthew 14:22–31). I am blown away by the Lord's response to Peter. Does Jesus chide impetuous Peter for his lack of faith? Does He give him a disgusted look? Does He tell him that because of his lack of faith he deserves to drown? Scripture records that the Master simply reaches out His hand and saves Peter from death by water.

Jesus does not rebuke the fearful disciple. He does not say, "Peter, You could have . . . , you should have . . . , you ought to have . . . , what's wrong with you?" None of that. Just a loving hand offers salvation from destruction. Peter quickly chooses. He doesn't hang his head in shame. He doesn't say to himself, "I deserve to drown." He doesn't hesitate because he can't be sure what the other disciples will think of him or say to him. He makes the wise choice: the hand of salvation. And because the Bible doesn't say that Jesus "beamed him" or carried him back into the boat, I think we can safely assume that Peter, with his faith in the living Word, continues to walk on water back to safety from the threatening waves.

Our Creator sees the big picture. Sometimes it's all we can do to see right past our noses, much less focus on a canvas that promises to stretch beyond our wildest dreams and imaginings. Even when we dare to peek at the canvas, the temptation to run the other way can capture us. If we muster the courage to choose the right path and start the journey, the temptation then is, all too often, to allow the circumstances of life to derail us.

It might be a wave of sickness or financial reversals; it might be a constant nagging insecurity or fear. It might be a storm of marital or family problems. It might be our own desires for recognition, financial success, and power that get out of control. Then, before we know it, we have allowed "the cares of this world, and the deceitfulness of riches, [or] the lusts of other things" to strangle God's Word and His plan for us (Mark 4:19).

"Pain is inevitable. Misery is optional." These words form the title of a book by Hyrum W. Smith (2004). They echo the meaning of words Jesus used when he warned His disciples present and those to come that they would encounter hardship and suffering. On the heels of that declaration, He gave them (and us) hope: "In the world ye shall have tribulation: but be of good cheer; I have overcome the world" (John 16:33). A more modern rendition of this verse says, "You will find trouble in the world—but, never lose heart, I have conquered the world!" (PHILLIPS). In other words, our Lord has deprived the world of its power to harm those who know and believe His Word and put their complete trust in Him.

As usual we have a choice. We can wallow around in the trouble and pain that characterize so much of life in this world and allow it to drown us and our influence, or we can choose to believe that God works out everything for our good (Romans 8:28). We don't have to succumb to the temptations, the hardships, the trials of life. We always control one variable. Though we may not always have control over the circumstances that threaten to engulf us, we do, however, have *complete* control over our responses to those circumstances. Our choices: respond in faith or respond in unbelief.

That choice sounds simple. It can be.

A Simple Choice?

An older couple without children might very well have challenged the simplicity of their choices a few centuries ago. About 1800 years BC (scholars have been unable to agree on an exact date), an older couple whose family was originally from Ur of the Chaldees, a region in what is currently known as Iraq, are engaged in life as usual. Their whole family, including the aging patriarch Terah, started a journey toward Canaan but stopped in Haran, about 600 miles away from the home they had left and close to an estimated 400 miles from the family's destination in Canaan. They seem to get stuck in Haran. It is there that the God of the universe speaks to one member of the family: God reveals to Abram, the son of Terah, His plan, His promises, and His provision.

Abram is married to Sarai at the time, but they are childless. Reared in a pagan culture among pagan families, Abram and Sarai find themselves without a biological heir. For Sarai, childless in a culture that measures a woman's worth by her ability to birth children, the lack of a child is unbearable. But the one true God speaks to Abram. Abram has already moved with his father and family to Haran on the way to Canaan. God's message to him puts him at a crossroads. He has a path to choose. Abram hears the voice of the one true God. He listens carefully.

> "Abram, leave your country and your kinfolk. Go to a land which I will show you; and I will make of you a great nation, and I will bless you and make your name great, and you shall be a blessing" (Genesis 12:1–5, my paraphrase).

"Abram, leave your family and your country."

"Okay."

"Abram, I'm not giving you the most up-to-date navigation system. I just want you to go; I'll reveal the way as you travel."

"Seriously, God?"

Abram, later to be called Abraham, is seventy-five years-old when God speaks these words to him. His wife is sixty-five. They have no children, but God promises He will bless their union and give them so many descendants that they will become a great nation:

> Now the Lord had said unto Abram, Get thee out of thy country, and from thy kindred, and from thy father's house, unto a land that I will shew thee: And I will make of thee a great nation, and I will bless thee, and make thy name great; and thou shalt be a blessing: And I will bless them that bless thee, and curse him that curseth thee: and in thee shall all families of the earth be blessed (Genesis 12:1–3).

They will be blessed and will be a blessing. Do they fully understand what that means? I wonder. Do we today understand God's promise to Abram and his descendants and later, by extension, to other believers that they will be blessed in the city and in the field, coming in and going out, in all of their activities and pursuits? (Deuteronomy 28)

At an age and a time in their lives when most of us today would be glad to settle down in a retirement community and sip lemonade on our front porches, Abram and his wife refuse to remain in the comfort of their complacency. They pack up all their belongings, gather about them their considerable wealth of animals and servants, and haul the freight out of Dodge, presumably on what our teens might call "BC Camelbacks." They move at God's command.

The Genesis story tells us that they begin their travel to an unknown destination. Eventually, God reveals their destination, and they make their way to Canaan. Because Abram believes what God told him, he obeys God's command. The perfect example of one who is willing to take God at His Word and do as He says regardless of what appears to be personal cost and loss to him, he moves out on faith, not on sight. He lives out Paul's reminder centuries later that "we walk by faith and not by sight" (2 Corinthians 5:7).

Scripture tells us that God notes Abram's faith and, because of that faith, God calls him righteous (a characteristic of someone who is just and has right standing with God). Think of that. Abram's faith and resulting obedience earn for him a distinguishing characteristic—righteousness—as well as the title Father of Faith. Because he believes God, Abram earns a place thousands of years later in the Faith Hall of Fame (Hebrews 11). In fact, he is a charter member.

According to the Bible, God promises that Abram will be blessed with land, that he will be father of a great nation, that his descendants will be as numerous as the stars in the heavens and the sands of the sea—impossible to number. When that promise comes to him, he is childless, and both he and his wife are old. They are both over the hill, reproductively speaking. What's worse, the two of them get in God's way. Just as many of us would do or may have done, they try to "help God."

After God's promise and nearly eleven years of continuing child-lessness, Sarai persuades Abram to have a child with her slave Hagar. Sarai has had plenty of time to figure it all out. Their cultural traditions will allow her to claim the child as her own, and they will be set. The promise will be fulfilled. Or so she thinks. They carry out her plan, and the child Ishmael is born. Unfortunately, joy and anticipation even-tually turn to sorrow and regret. Scripture doesn't say so specifically, but I can imagine that Hagar taunted Sarai behind Abram's back. The child Ishmael, instead of becoming son of Sarai, must have reminded the childless woman of her barrenness. Abram and Sarai were no better off than when God had given the promise so many years before. The world would, in the long run, be much worse off.

With a new child in the household, life goes on for Mr. and Mrs. Abram. They continue life as usual, not questioning the wisdom of God and His direction. A little more than twenty-four years after His promise to Abram, God renews the promise. This time He tells Abram that his son with Sarai will be born at "the set time." At this meeting, God changes his name to Abraham (meaning father of a great mul-titude), and He also gives Sarai (meaning quarrelsome in Hebrew, Princess in the Bible) the new name of Sarah (meaning my Princess).

From that day forward, Abraham speaks his faith every time he has to introduce himself to someone. As he says, "My name is Abraham," he is effectively saying, "I am the father of a great multitude." And this is the man who, as yet, has no child by Sarah. He is ninety-nine years old. He has only one child and that one by a slave. But in the fullness of God's perfect timing, God fulfills His promise. Human machinations do not bring it to pass. God does! Abraham is one hundred years old and Sarah is ninety when the promised child makes his appearance. They name the promise Isaac.

After the birth of Isaac, trouble erupts between the two women in Abraham's life because of the two children. Life in the Abraham household seems to have become intolerable for Abraham as well as Sarah. Tempers fester. An explosion waits for the right spark. That spark is not long in coming. At the time of the weaning of Isaac, Abraham throws a party, a celebration feast. During the party, Sarah notes that Ishmael is mocking. Angered by his actions, Sarah determines that Isaac will not share his inheritance with the son of the bondwoman; she makes demands of Abraham. God supports her demands.

Sarah, with God's approval, forces Abraham to evict his concubine and his own child. Greatly troubled by this move, Abraham grieves the loss of his firstborn. During his grief, faithful God speaks comfort, assurance, and another promise to him:

> "Let it not be grievous in thy sight because of the lad,
> and because of thy bondwoman; in all that Sarah hath
> said unto thee, hearken unto her voice; for in Isaac shall
> thy seed be called. And also of the son of the bond-
> woman will I make a nation, because he is thy seed."
> (Genesis 21:12–13)

Abraham has a choice when he is still Abram. He can choose to believe in the one true God and follow Him or He can doubt that the "voice" he hears is that of Almighty God. He can choose to doubt. However, he exercises his faith while he is still Abram and finds that God is faithful. Abraham's faith determines his destiny.

By the same token, our choice—faith in God and His Word or doubt and unbelief—will determine our destiny.

Abraham and Sarah experience God's faithfulness even in the midst of their muddling efforts to bring God's promises to pass. Centuries later, people all over the world somewhat playfully blame Abraham and Sarah for the problems in the Middle East between the descendants of the two children of Abraham. The man of God who came to be called the Father of Faith had no way of knowing what trouble would result many years later from their choices.

While Scripture does not depict Abraham as perfect, it does emphasize the important characteristic of Abraham: his faith. Centuries later, the writer of Hebrews notes the strong faith of Abraham and Sarah:

> By faith Abraham, when he was called to go out into a place which he should after receive for an inheritance, obeyed; and he went out, not knowing whither he went. By faith he sojourned in the land of promise, as in a strange country, dwelling in tabernacles [tents] with Isaac and Jacob, the heirs with him of the same promise: For he looked for a city which hath foundations, whose builder and maker is God. Through faith also Sara herself received strength to conceive seed, and was delivered of a child when she was past age, because she judged him faithful who had promised. Therefore sprang there even of one, and him as good as dead, so many as the stars of the sky in multitude, and as the sand which is by the sea shore innumerable (Hebrews 11:8–12).

Today, because of the example of this couple, we can conclude several truths: (1) God keeps His promises; (2) God's timetable is not ours; (3) Patience possesses the promises; (4) Consult God before making choices; they could impact many generations—not only of our descendants but perhaps a much wider circle than we can possibly imagine.

Chapter 19

ENTERING THE HOME STRETCH

I press toward the mark for the prize of the high calling of God in
Christ Jesus.
–Philippians 3:14

———◆———

Recently, our son paid me a somewhat backhanded compliment. As we were leaving a restaurant after lunch, Larry commented, "Mom you look nice today. I really like your outfit."

Hmm. I liked that. I had little time to relish that compliment before he blasted me.

"Not bad for an old lady."

Immediately, my spirit balloon rose only to sink a notch or two. Old? Me? I don't think of myself as old. Why, I'm not as old as Moses who, at eighty, began the forty-year journey with the children of Israel from bondage in Egypt to freedom and a long trek toward the promised Land. I'm also nowhere near the age of Caleb (85) when he asked Joshua to let him have the mountain with its great walled cities held by giants (Joshua 14:6–15). To me, age is a state of mind, and I don't think "old."

However, some truth rang in his words. I have to admit that I'm old by many standards, but not until I look in the mirror do I see old. My inner being is alive, vibrant, eager to learn more about Jesus and become more like Him. As I look back on my life's journey, I realize the Lord has brought me a long way. God began His work in me when I was a child, but, like Paul, I can't say I have arrived:

> I don't mean to say that I have already achieved these
> things or that I have already reached perfection. But
> I press on to possess that perfection for which Christ

Jesus first possessed me. No, dear brothers and sisters, I have not achieved it, but I focus on this one thing: Forgetting the past and looking forward to what lies ahead, I press on to reach the end of the race and receive the heavenly prize for which God, through Christ Jesus, is calling us. (Philippians 3:12–14 NLT)

Paul's word choices suggest that his Christian "race" continues to compel him to push himself forward, as if by force, to the finish line to which God has called him. Your race and mine require the same determination which Paul showed. His words challenge us to keep looking forward, to keep reaching, to keep on pressing past the milestones God reveals before us so that we can fulfill His will for our lives.

While I was practicing "religion," I found myself living without what A. W. Tozer calls "holy desire" (christianquotes.info). I was too consumed with keeping the rules and "doing the right thing." Thinking it was the right thing to do, I allowed my Christian teachers and mentors to do the seeking and understanding for me. And because I didn't know for too many years that I could be free, I continued in bondage to checklists, fear of God, fear of judgment, fear of being weighed in the balances and found wanting, fear of dying and going to hell. I believed I needed to work my way to heaven, but I could never find peace about how much work is enough.

What I didn't realize is that all the while I was practicing what I knew and understood of the Scripture, God was illuminating for me more of His will. I was actually fulfilling the promise I made the first time I joined a church: "to walk in the light as it shines on my pathway." The more "light" I received on the Bible and the more I tried to walk in it, the more conflicted I became. I won't claim, as some do, that God gave me a "new" revelation. I firmly believe the revelation of God I now have has been in the Bible all the time; it's there for all to see, so it's not God's fault that I walked in ignorance or partial darkness. It's not His fault if that is where you are. I can say today that "noise" impeded my hearing, my seeing, and my understanding; it was the noise of opinions, traditions, misunderstandings, no reading or lack of careful reading, reading out of context, or complacency. What was true for me might be true for you too. Many barriers to our spiritual understanding plague us throughout life, but I have good news. We can allow the Holy Spirit to reveal the barriers and to help us sprint around them, through them, or over them, much as a world-class athlete manages an obstacle course.

After many years of clinging devoutly to what I had been taught, I learned that God used Moses and the prophet Micah to spell out pretty clearly what He requires of us. The requirements say nothing about a checklist of Dos and Don'ts. We find the instructions of Moses in Deuteronomy 10:12–13:

> And now, Israel, what doth the LORD thy God require
> of thee, but to fear the LORD thy God, to walk in all
> his ways, and to love him, and to serve the LORD thy
> God with all thy heart and with all thy soul, To keep the
> commandments of the LORD, and his statutes, which
> I command thee this day for thy good?

God instructed Moses to tell His people the four things He asks of those who follow Him:

1. Fear Him. Couple that fear with holy reverence and awe.
2. Walk the path He chooses for you.
3. Love and serve Him with your heart and soul.
4. Keep His commandments and laws.

A few hundred years later, we find the prophet Micah saying, "the Lord has told you what is good, and this is what he requires of you: to do what is right, to love mercy, and to walk humbly with your God" (Micah 6:8 NLT).

1. Be fair and do what's right.
2. Love others and practice compassion.
3. Humble yourself before God.

But Jesus covered the instructions of both Moses and Micah when He condensed the Ten Commandments for the Pharisees and Saducees into the two great commandments: "Thou shalt love the Lord thy God with all thy heart, and with all thy soul, and with all thy mind. This is the first and great commandment. And the second is like unto it, Thou shalt love thy neighbor thyself" (Matthew 22:37–39).

1. Love God with everything that is in you: heart, soul, and mind.
2. Love your neighbor as yourself.

Love is the key word. Love God first; then love your neighbor. Who is your neighbor? People asked that question centuries ago. They still ask it. The story of the Good Samaritan, recorded in Luke 10:25–37, defines *neighbor* as whoever shows mercy to someone in need, whether they are part of your social, economic, cultural, or religious group or not.

The instructions are so simple that you may have trouble believing that's all God requires. But think about it. If you love God with your whole heart, that's going to take care of honoring Him and His Word. It will assure that you worship no other gods, that you put Him first in your life, that you obey what He says. Then, if you love others as much as you love yourself, you will treat them and everything that belongs to them with mercy and grace, with respect and fairness. You will walk out your love in every aspect of your life. If you're not there yet, there's hope. Put your confidence in your ability to arrive, *not* in yourself, but in Christ. He empowers us to do what He calls us to do. Every. Time.

The move from legalism to grace has not been without its challenges. It has consumed most of my life; actually, it didn't even start until the second half of my life. It has been an arduous journey in many ways because the rules and traditions were such an ingrained part of me. Before I learned to love God, I learned to fear Him. Before I learned that I could trust the Holy Spirit to give me understanding of the Bible, I trusted my preachers and teachers who could teach only what they knew. My knowledge was limited to the understanding of other people, people who loved God, for the most part. In a few cases, people who were saved, sanctified, and satisfied with the status quo served as my guides. But in spite of being surrounded and almost inundated with people's ideas and opinions, I learned a few things that continue to inform my life and spiritual walk.

I learned early to trust God with small things and to look to Him to answer prayer. Just as David learned that he could trust God to help him kill the lions and the bears that threatened his father's sheep before he faced the giant (I Samuel 17:34–37), I learned to call on God as a child under my mother's and my grandmother's example. I first trusted Him with problems like my dad's safety after accidents, my little sister's near-death experience, headaches, upset stomach, earaches, and our baby's next meal. I asked Him for help with my school work and did all the studying that I needed for success. Then, after trusting Him with smaller things, it was not as difficult to look to the Lord for the more "major" needs of my life—the illnesses, the times of financial leanness, the disappointments, the heartbreak of deaths among family and friends. The same thing can be true for you.

Our Bible teaches us that God shows no favoritism. Peter says that God is no "respecter of persons" (Acts 10:34) and Paul also emphasizes the same point (Romans 2:11). We understand that, in context, Peter has recognized that the message of Jesus Christ and His gift of life belongs not only to the Jews but also to the Gentiles. Paul, on the other hand speaks of God's applying justice and mercy equally to all people. I believe that their words also apply to the life situations of every person who believes in Jesus: what God has done for others, He'll do for you and me. The key to receiving from God is *faith*, complete trust in and reliance on Him.

You don't even have to worry about not having faith. God's Word says that He assigns or distributes to every believer the "measure of faith" (Romans 12:3), an ability to rely completely on and put our full confidence in Him. To exercise that faith, you begin by talking to and listening to God about what you may consider minor things before you are thrust into a situation where you need to exercise great faith. If you start with the smaller, less important issues in your life, you will learn beyond any doubt that God answers prayers for you. That knowledge, along with a treasure of Word stored inside you built by hearing and hearing and hearing the Word (Romans 10:17), will help take you to the next level. with help from the Holy Spirit, that stored Word will be available when you need it, and your faith will be stronger. As Jesus promises: "But the Comforter, which is the Holy Ghost, whom the Father will send in my name, he shall teach you all things, and bring all things to your remembrance, whatsoever I have said unto you." (John 14:26)

Will you indulge me as I point out the obvious? We first have to know what the Word says before the Comforter can bring it back to our memory. We can't really know it unless we have spent time with the Word—reading it, asking for divine understanding of it, thinking about it, meditating on it, speaking it, writing it. God's words to Joshua many centuries ago provide supernatural instruction and inspiration for us today as we earnestly learn God's Word:

"This book of the law shall not depart out of thy mouth;
but thou shalt meditate therein day and night, that thou

mayest observe to do according to all that is written therein: for then thou shalt make thy way prosperous, and then thou shalt have good success." (Joshua 1:8)

What is the Lord actually saying to Joshua? He is instructing Moses' replacement how to be successful in leading the children of Israel into the Promised Land after the death of Moses. His instructions were and still are simple. (1) Speak the Word of God. Hear it coming out of your mouth over and over. (2) Meditate on it constantly. When He says "meditate on it day and night," He is telling Joshua to do more than just to think about it all the time. The Hebrew word translated *meditate* also means "to mutter or mumble, to speak, to recite" (Strong's Concordance). Then, (3) Do all it says to do. Finally, God tells Joshua, in effect, As you keep the book of the law fresh in your memory by speaking it over and over to yourself and doing all that's written in it, you'll succeed where Moses failed. The instructions to Joshua will also lead us to success in our walk with the Lord if we practice what God told Joshua to do.

If you have come this far with me, then I pray you will not regret the time you have put into sharing my journey. Hopefully, you have been inspired to enlarge your borders, to dare to reach for goals you may have abandoned, to stretch spiritually. You may not agree with all my conclusions, but that's not a problem. You may question or disdain my theology, but I've tried to give you plenty of God's Word to remember or to chew on and digest. Sometimes our quest for truth needs a kick start. Maybe you got that.

God uses many different means to help us to grow spiritually: the words of the Bible, shared Scripture from preachers and Bible teachers, exposition and encouragement in print or video, conversations with friends and your family of choice (others who love God), the still small voice of the Holy Spirit—maybe even this book. My closing hope is that something I've written has enriched your spirit and fanned the hope that is within you: That you follow the leading of the Lord. That you allow Him to stretch you to fit His pattern and His will. That you leave behind all the weights that can entangle you and finish your race with patient endurance (Hebrews 12:1). May your journey take you where God wants you, not where you think you might be or should be headed. May His overwhelming, matchless love support and sustain you as you walk with Him into all that He has for you.